"Tenshin Reb Anderson, one of the most important Zen teachers of our age, places the famous *Lotus Sutra* parable of the lost and destitute child at the center of a matrix of teachings that guide the reader to a realization of one's true nature and original home. As he develops this text, he weaves in marvelous anecdotes from his own long, adventurous, and dedicated life, demonstrating how deeply he understands what it means to be a 'destitute' and wandering child, spiritually. His commentary is both clear and subtle, not falling into prescriptions for practice, yet lighting the way to recognizing the bodhisattva path to one's own homecoming."

—KONJIN GAELYN GODWIN,
abbot of Houston Zen Center and Auspicious Cloud Temple,
director of Soto Zen Buddhism North America International Center

"This powerful book is a profound and timeless offering to all practitioners of the dharma, and truly for all of us who are committed to end suffering in our world in a non-transactional way. As Tenshin Anderson shows us, 'Bodhisattvas have nothing to attain and everything to realize.' This is a courageous and wise call in today's world, a call that is important for us to heed. As the author's second dharma name, *Zenki*, reflects, this is 'the whole works.'"

—ROSHI JOAN HALIFAX,
abbot of Upaya Zen Center, Santa Fe, New Mexico

"Reb Anderson's beautifully written book takes perhaps the most important 'meta-koan' of Zen practice—that beneath all of our ardent striving there is actually *nothing to attain*—as a guide through a series of wonderful stories, illuminating many of the most salient dimensions of the Buddhist path. This is clearly a book arising out of decades of profound practice and insightful teaching."

—DALE WRIGHT,
professor emeritus of religious studies and Asian studies,
Occidental College, author of *What Is Buddhist Enlightenment?*

"A voice of upright Zen, Tenshin Reb Anderson Roshi spectacularly reflects his life story of authentic practicing and teaching Zen meditation, which I have closely witnessed for fifty years."

—KAZUAKI TANAHASHI, editor of *Treasury of the True Dharma Eye: Zen Master Dogen's Shobo Genzo*

"By weaving together tales of his own practice in Suzuki Shunryu's lineage with *Lotus Sutra* parables and reflections on a bodhisattva's teachings and training methods offered by Dogen, Dongshan, and numerous other traditional luminaries, Reb Anderson's new book is a fascinating and insightful account of how leading the Zen life becomes an ongoing experience of discovery about one's true inner self or original face. Several decades in the making, *Nothing to Attain* unlocks the profound mystery of why Suzuki once instructed that his student's dharma name, Tenshin, means 'Reb is Reb,' as well as the many intriguing ways in which Anderson rejoices today in this continuously renewed understanding."

—STEVEN HEINE, director of the Asian studies program, Florida International University, and author of *Dogen: Japan's Original Zen Teacher*

"I recommend this book to all bodhisattvas practicing Soto Zen. I am glad that the dharma flower of the tree transplanted by Dogen Zenji in Japan is now blooming in the cultural soil of America. Bodhisattva practice is a journey to return home, where we are from. When we arrive home, we intimately practice with our teacher to inherit the Buddha's wealth. Anderson Roshi clearly describes the process using many lively stories that reveal the family treasure from Suzuki Roshi."

—SHOHAKU OKUMURA, former abbot of Sanshinji Zen Community, Bloomington, Indiana

"*Nothing to Attain* describes the inner workings of the Buddha Way, a treasure to inform all practitioners. As a central metaphor, Reb Anderson celebrates the prodigal son from the *Lotus Sutra*, who must shovel dung in his father's fields until ready for his birthright. This metaphor echoes all our situations, born to the forgotten nobility of awakening in which we contain everything in the universe, and vice versa. There's nothing separate to gain. Reb describes many personal anecdotes, from childhood through study with Suzuki Roshi to his years as abbot. For example, for Suzuki Roshi, a young Reb moved slightly a large rock in a garden all day, only for it to end up where it started. Reb cites many traditional koans, especially Yangshan's, invoking the stage of faith and stage of person. We all are awakened from the beginning, only needing to realize this reality beyond our personal karmic entanglements."

—TAIGEN DAN LEIGHTON, guiding teacher emeritus of Ancient Dragon Zen Gate, peace activist, and author of *Just This Is It: Dongshan and the Practice of Suchness*, *Dogen's Extensive Record*, and *Cultivating the Empty Field: The Silent Illumination of Buddhist Master Hongzhi*

"Be ready to work side by side with Reb Anderson as he compassionately shows us the way to shovel dung, muck out the stalls, and embody the practice revealed in the *Lotus Sutra*'s parable of the destitute child. Reb celebrates this parable and other Zen stories in deep and thorough conversation, often including intimate stories of practice life with his teacher, Shunryu Suzuki Roshi. In this way, Reb uncovers the family jewels and the mystery of the truth that there is *nothing to attain*—that our rich inheritance, our family treasure, is waiting for us to come home straightaway and receive it. 'Haven't you heard that the family jewels do not come through the front gate?'"

—LINDA RUTH CUTTS, former abbess of San Francisco Zen Center

"Nearly sixty years ago, Tenshin Reb Anderson stepped into a place of wonder called the San Francisco Zen Center. Inside the entry way was his teacher, Shunryu Suzuki Roshi, dressed all in black, silently and slowly walking toward the Zendo. *Left foot, right foot . . . left foot, right foot.* Having now written an account of his own travels through the wonderland of Zen in the footsteps of his teacher, Tenshin Roshi has chosen for us a story from the *Lotus Sutra* as a travel guide for that same journey. *What are we going to find in a land where there is nothing to find?* For me, a heartfelt gratitude for my own teacher living within the light of Suzuki Roshi's awakened vision."

—FURYU NANCY SCHROEDER,
former abiding abbess at Green Gulch Farm

"Do you want to learn how to illuminate consciousness by shoveling dung? Would you like to find out how sluggish birds and exhausted fish become cranes and dragons? Do you wish to see delusion and wisdom intimately dancing together and liberating each other? If so, read this book. But don't try to attain anything!"

—LINDA HESS,
senior lecturer emerita of religious studies,
Stanford University

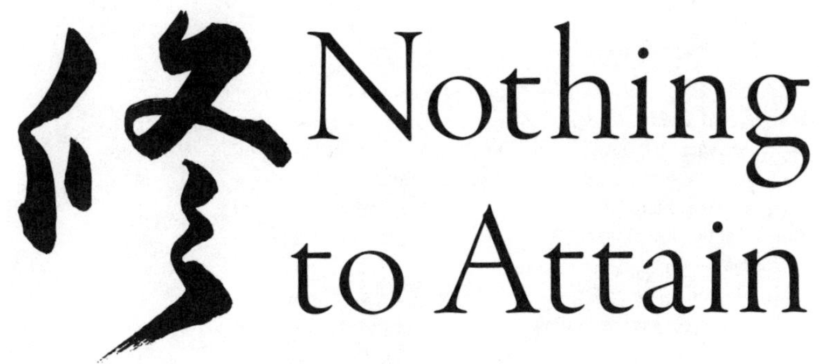

Nothing to Attain

ZEN STORIES OF FAITH AND UNDERSTANDING

Reb Anderson

SHAMBHALA

Shambhala Publications, Inc.
2129 13th Street
Boulder, Colorado 80302
www.shambhala.com

Cover art: Poem by Akazome Emon, from the series *One Hundred Poems Explained by the Nurse* (*Hyakunin isshu uba ga etoki*), Katsushika Hokusai.
Gift of Mrs. Carll Tucker, 1962.
Cover design: Daniel Urban-Brown

9 8 7 6 5 4 3 2 1

First Edition
Printed in the United States of America

Shambhala Publications makes every effort to print on acid-free, recycled paper.
Shambhala Publications is distributed worldwide by Penguin Random House, Inc., and its subsidiaries.

LIBRARY OF CONGRESS CATALOGING-IN-PUBLICATION DATA
Names: Anderson, Reb author
Title: Nothing to attain: Zen stories of faith and understanding / Reb Anderson.
Description: Boulder, Colorado: Shambhala [2026] | Includes bibliographical references.
Identifiers: LCCN 2025017805 | ISBN 9781645474272 trade paperback
Subjects: LCSH: Spiritual life—Zen Buddhism
Classification: LCC BQ9288 .A5195 2026 | DDC 294.3/444—dc23/eng/20250909
LC record available at https://lccn.loc.gov/2025017805

The authorized representative in the EU for product safety and compliance is eucomply OÜ, Pärnu mnt 139b-14, 11317 Tallinn, Estonia, hello@eucompliancepartner.com.

Homage to our great original, beneficent teacher Shakyamuni Buddha.

Homage to all the ancestors who have transmitted the family business of bodhisattvas face-to-face.

Homage to all those who wish to realize awakening to liberate all beings so that they may dwell in peace and harmony in this world of suffering.

My sincere wish is that this book will aid and inspire the reader to realize the truth of the Buddha Way.

I pray that it will support their study of the stories of our ancestors and the discovery of the jewels hidden within them.

I pray that these stories in this book and our discussion of them will help the reader explore the bodhisattva vows and practices and enable them to enter the house of Buddha.

I pray that all beings will realize their original nature.

CONTENTS

PREFACE AND ACKNOWLEDGMENTS

THIS IS A BOOK OF STORIES. In our Zen family, we receive and transmit the bodhisattva vows to save all living beings. The stories in this book are about people practicing to realize these vows. However, the members of a family do not necessarily agree with all of the traditions of the family or completely understand the wishes of their parents and ancestors. The point of these stories is to maintain the vitality and intimacy of the family even when its members disagree or would like to try something unprecedented.

How can we hold our family and community together in the midst of diverse views and disagreement under ever-changing circumstances? One way to protect and maintain family and community is by transmitting and sharing really good family stories. I will attempt to do so in this book. I will not tell you what you are going to learn from this book, but I will tell you about my understanding of the bodhisattva vows, about the vows that I feel in my own life, and about the path of training embodied in our Zen family.

Here is a story about how the book came to be and all those generous people who contributed to it.

From about 1987 to 2004, I met together with groups of enthusiastic Zen students to study a classic text called the *Book of Serenity*, a collection of one hundred ancient stories of Chinese Zen teachers' intimate conversations with their students. We studied and practiced with these stories in many different ways, including reading, reciting, memorizing, dharma discussions, and dramatic enactments. During these meetings we focused on training in awakening to intimacy as it is taught in those ancient stories. In this wondrous course of study, we were filled with joy and gratitude.

Afterward, some of the members of our group transcribed and edited the audio recordings of these meetings. Charlie Pokorny started transcribing these recordings in the 1990s. The transcripts were then offered to me as possible resource materials for creating a book on Zen training and practice. I accepted this gift and have endeavored to be a caretaker of this material ever since.

After looking at these transcripts again and again, I tried to imagine a framework, a matrix, that could accommodate and illuminate the different aspects of practice that were included in the various stories and in our conversations. This wondering went on for years. I wanted to repay the great kindness, generosity, and devotion of the transcribers and editors by bringing all their work to fruition as a book that would benefit many beings. I struggled with this responsibility for some time.

Finally, I experienced an epiphany. I remembered that an ancient teacher said that the parable of the destitute child in the *Lotus Sutra* illustrates the path of awakening. It seemed to me that this parable from the *Lotus Sutra* could serve as an all-embracing framework for the process of Zen training in awakening as expressed in the stories from the *Book of Serenity* and embodied in the conversations of our community.

Catherine Gammon began editing the transcripts about twenty years ago at Green Gulch Farm. She focused on editing the transcripts of teachings that were offered in Case 32 in the *Book of Serenity*. Eventually this effort yielded a manuscript of a hundred pages or so, devoted just to this single case. It was a deeply fruitful process of study for her but incomplete as a book. An effort to combine that material with teachings on contemporary priest training followed but didn't cohere as a book. I can only hint at my gratitude and appreciation for Catherine's devotion to this project. She generously brought her great literary and critical skills to the editorial process. For a long time after this, the manuscript rested. In 2016, Catherine resumed working on it and shared her work with me. I read and contemplated this work; however, I was still unable to see how all this material could come together as a book.

Then in 2019 I had the epiphany about the *Lotus Sutra* parable described above. With this epiphany, I went back to work on the material that Catherine had given me. At that time, I invited another skilled writer and editor, Eleanor Howe, to help in adapting the Zen stories into the framework of the parable in hopes that it would soon be a book. She worked with me for about three years. When I think of Eleanor's bright, patient, and penetrating work, I am filled with appreciation, gratitude, and respect.

Around 2020, I invited Karen Mueller, who had worked with me on a previous book, *Entering the Mind of Buddha*, to join this process of fleshing out this basic structure for the new book. In particular, the introduction through chapter 5 and chapters 10 through 13 were developed through many hours of conversation with her. She encouraged me to find and bring in my personal experience into the context of the parable again and again. She also kept a watchful eye on how the elements of the *Lotus Sutra* story were illustrated in the stories from the *Book of Serenity* and on the chronology of the personal stories. We worked together to bring the *Lotus Sutra* parable into the discussion of the other traditional and personal stories that make up the final chapters of the book. In this process, she offered feedback, questions, and her understanding of this material and attempted to anticipate and clarify questions that might come up for the readers.

After the manuscript was fleshed out, Catherine Gammon read it again in its entirety and provided substantive and insightful feedback. Bert Dyer and Marie Ferreboeuf also read earlier versions of the full manuscript and provided helpful questions and suggestions. I thank them both for their time and thoughtful contributions. All of their suggestions and questions were gratefully incorporated in the final form of this book.

Once the book was accepted for publication, Karen continued to be involved in the final editing of the manuscript and assisted me with researching the accuracy of quotations and obtaining the necessary permissions for their use, along with the other more technical aspects involved in bringing this book to publication.

Although the words offered in this book are, in a sense, coming from me, without Karen's support and encouragement, this book would not have reached completion. She has been an indefatigable cheerleader and graciously brought out things I might not have noticed and helped me to address those concerns. If this turns out to be a book that is of some benefit in the world and guides and encourages people in awakening and in realizing the bodhisattva vows, Karen is to be deeply thanked for her work.

I also sincerely thank Nikko Odiseos, the president of Shambhala Publications, for his support in bringing this book to publication. I had the opportunity to meet Nikko at a birthday party, and he asked me if I had any books that I was working on. I told him about this project, and he graciously encouraged me to send it to him at Shambhala. With his support, the manuscript was accepted for publication, and Peter Schumacher became our editor at Shambhala. Peter brought his own knowledge and experience of Buddhism, along with his encouragement, kindness, and thoughtful questions to this project. Peter also made himself available to respond to our questions quickly throughout this entire process, which greatly facilitated the work.

Now the time has come for me to express a little bit of my immense gratitude for my wife, Rusa Chiu. In the autumn of 1971 as Suzuki Roshi was dying, we met in a graduate seminar on the *Lotus Sutra* at UC Berkeley led by the great Buddhist scholar Edward Conze. I noticed her, but I didn't know if she had noticed me; but from that time on until the present, Rusa has been intimately involved in my practice and study of the buddhadharma. She has sincerely and devotedly supported me in so many ways. No one knows the full extent of it. When she sees me studying, she often expresses appreciation for my strange behavior. She says, "You are so fortunate. Your profession, your vocation, and your hobby are all the same." How auspicious! How auspicious! How auspicious!

NOTHING TO ATTAIN

INTRODUCTION

The Parable of the Destitute Child

IN THE WONDROUS FLOWER ADORNMENT SCRIPTURE (*Avatamsaka Sutra*),[1] the Buddha tells us, "Now I see that all living beings fully possess the wisdom and virtues of the buddhas. However, because of misconceptions and attachments, they do not realize it." Because we do not realize this, someone has to tell us. The Buddha reveals that we have the resources of the buddhas' wisdom and virtue to serve all beings. Fully possessing the wisdom and virtues of the buddhas is our original inheritance. In this teaching, there is nothing for us to attain *and* we have to engage in the great work of dropping off misconceptions and attachments.

This teaching and all the teachings in this sutra are offered for bodhisattvas. And who are the bodhisattvas? Some say that bodhisattvas are those in whom a great vow has arisen to realize buddhahood for the welfare of all beings. Others say that we are all bodhisattvas whether we know it or not. When some people hear about the bodhisattva aspiration to realize buddhahood for the benefit of the world, they might say, "I'm sorry but I don't aspire to buddhahood. That's too much for me." They may appreciate and even admire the bodhisattva way, but they don't feel confident and ready to express the aspiration or feel ready to even think about entering into a training program to realize the awakening of buddhas.

Although many people sincerely wish to live for the welfare of the world, they may not have the faith and understanding that the bodhisattva aspiration is appropriate for them. Even those who do have this great aspiration still need to enter into study and training to become free of the afflictions of misconceptions and attachments. In this way, our aspiration is purified. Through training, we will realize our inheritance of the wisdom and virtues of the buddhas. For me, this is the purification of our love, the point of Zen training.

For this purpose, we will consider a parable from the *Lotus Sutra* found in a chapter called "Faith and Understanding." The main and unique teaching of the *Lotus Sutra* is that we are all on the same path. All beings are bodhisattvas on the path to buddhahood. In China and Japan this scripture is perhaps the most venerated and studied in the vast ocean of Buddhist scriptures.

This parable addresses the same situation described in the *Avatamsaka Sutra*. It is a story about a child who wanders away from his home and finally returns. It lays out an overall structure for the path of bodhisattva training, culminating in understanding our original nature.

In this chapter, Shakyamuni Buddha predicts the buddhahood of five hundred assembled disciples. After hearing this inspiring and profoundly surprising news, the Buddha's great disciples dance for joy. To express their joy and gratitude to the Buddha for this amazing gift, which they have never received before, and to explain how they feel about it, they tell the Buddha the following parable:

The Parable of the Destitute Child

Once there was a child who wandered away from his original home and became lost. The more he wandered the poorer and needier he became. This child wandered for about fifty years before he, by chance, encountered his father's home.

All this time, the father searched unsuccessfully for his child. At the same time, the father's household became wealthy and overflowed with treasures, and they now lived in a different city from where the family had originally resided.

Although this child was lost for more than fifty years, the father thought about him all the time, but he never spoke of his son to anyone. He only thought to himself, "Old and tired out, I have great wealth, gold and silver and rare treasures overflowing my storehouses. And yet I have no child to inherit this. Someday my end will come, and my estate will be scattered and lost, for there is no one to whom I can leave it. If I could only get him back and entrust my wealth to him, how contented, how happy I would be, with no more anxiety."

Finally, after drifting from one place to another, the poor son accidentally arrived at his father's house. Standing at the gate, he saw his father from a distance, seated on a lion throne surrounded by great scholars, warriors, and householders and attended by many servants. His father looked majestic and distinguished. Seeing such great power and wealth, the poor son was seized by fear. He thought, "That person must be a king or something like a king. This is no place for me to try to make a living. I'd better go to some poorer town, where I can be paid for my labor and where it will be easier to get food and clothing. If I stay here, I may be captured and forced to work as a slave." Thinking these thoughts, he ran away.

The elderly father on the lion throne recognized his son at first sight but didn't tell the others. Filled with joy, he thought, "At last I see the one to whom my stores of wealth are to be entrusted. Old and worn out, I yearned for an heir. I thought of him always but had no way to find him. Now suddenly he has come by himself! My hopes are completely fulfilled."

He sent messengers to bring back his son. When they took hold of him firmly, the son was surprised and terrified. He cried out, "I have done nothing wrong!" Thinking they would either capture him and put him into slavery or kill him, he fainted.

The father saw this and understood what was going on. He called his messengers back. He told them, "Let him go. Don't force him to come. Sprinkle some cold water on his face to wake him up and say nothing more about this." The father understood that his son's ambitions were limited and that the family inheritance would be too difficult for the son to accept in his present state. The messengers told the son, "We are releasing you. You are free to go wherever you want," and the poor son rejoiced in having obtained what he had not had before. He got up and went off in search of food and clothing.

Then the father, wanting to entice his son back, thought of a skillful means. He sent men of humble appearance dressed in torn, dirty rags to his son. When they caught up with the son, they offered him work shoveling dung in the stables of his father's estate. The poor son was happy with this offer, but he was still worried that he would be put into slavery, so he asked for an advance on his pay, and then he went to work.

The son worked in this way for a long time, and eventually, his father went to visit him in the stables, also dressed in dirty, ragged clothes. Seeing that his son was enjoying these menial tasks, the father spoke to him rather gruffly but praised his work. He saw how diligently his son was working and commended him for not being lazy or deceitful, grouchy or angry. He asked him to stay and work there, and he assured his son that he didn't have to worry about needing anything. He told him, "I have observed your good actions and from now on, you shall be like my own son."

He encouraged his son and gradually increased his wages and gave him a new name, as one would to a child. The son was pleased but still considered himself to be a lowly person. For many years, he continued to clear dung and live as a laborer. By shoveling the dung in exchange for food and clothing, his confidence gradually grew.

Then the old father became ill, and knowing that he would die soon, he summoned his son to the house. He said to the son, "I want you to learn the comings and goings and the business of the house and to become knowledgeable about this realm of great abundance. And what is my reason? It is that you and I are now to be no different."

The father offered him a position of responsibility within the household, and the son was now ready to accept this position. While he had initially been afraid to be near the house, he now dared to enter it, but he still considered himself to be a lowly person. As he learned the ways of the house, the son also became closer to his father, but he still didn't know that this person was actually his father.

Finally, the father saw that his son had become more confident and skilled and that he had let go of his former sense of inferiority. The time had arrived for the father to gather together leaders of the country and all his acquaintances to announce to them, "This man is actually my son. I entrust everything to him." The son was now ready to accept this entrustment and rejoiced in receiving something he had never had before. Without any intention to obtain them, these treasures came to the son of themselves.[2]

Guided by the parable of the destitute child, we will explore the process of Zen practice and realization throughout this book. Like the child, we also have an original home from which we have wandered away. We vaguely sense that we have such a home but because we do not know that for sure, we feel lost and yearn for it. Motivated by yearning, we wander away from where we are into destitution, but we are always, consciously or unconsciously, looking for our original home. In the process of this foolish search, we miraculously reencounter our original home and family, but when we do, we are not ready to reengage with them.

In this state of unreadiness, like the poor child, we are kindly offered expedient practices that train us to accept and reengage with this great opportunity. In the beginning, as in the parable, we engage in forms of training called dung shoveling. Dung shoveling is a metaphor for the initial training of a bodhisattva. In this training, we learn to thoroughly investigate the confusion and alienation of our egocentric consciousness. In this process, we come to know the true characteristics of this self-centeredness and become free of it. As our confidence grows through these practices, we become ready to enter the house and transition to the real selfless practice of the buddhas, which is our family business. Within this practice, we realize the nonduality of these initial expedient practices and the real practice of all buddhas.

The *Lotus Sutra* predicts that we will enter our original home and awaken to our true family. When we realize and accept our true home, we will not wander away again. We will also understand that, in reality, we have always been in this home and family throughout the entire course of our training. We will understand what our family business is. We will be able to take care of it and transmit it to all living beings past, present, and future.

We will see that we come from abundance, and yet we must enter into poverty to develop the skills we need to fulfill our original nature. Our true home is not sagehood or ordinariness. Our great, original wealth is the harmony of sagehood and ordinariness, the nonduality of poverty and abundance. Leaping beyond both, we actualize our original home.

The original wealth and inheritance of all living beings must plunge into poverty to manifest itself. When we understand this original wealth, we will be stimulated to engage in the work of sharing it so that all beings will be free of both poverty and wealth. In this realization, we learn that poverty and wealth are inseparable. This allows us to embrace and bring blessings to all forms of poverty and wealth. We must wander into poverty and fear to verify that poverty and fear live in all forms of wealth and safety.

The words *wealth* and *poverty* carry a strong charge and many painful associations in our world today. If we don't acknowledge this, it might seem that we are not deeply concerned and troubled by the inequities and injustices that surround us and the terrible inequalities of wealth and privilege. As bodhisattvas we are called to face and address the myriad forms of injustice and oppression with regard to humans, animals, plants, and the whole environment.

We might wonder how this story from the *Lotus Sutra* addresses and repairs the terrible mental and physical suffering, inequality, and injustice of our world. How does the parable of the destitute child help us to realize our original home and enable us to work for freedom and equality among all beings? How does this story support and guide us in questioning all forms of social and environmental injustice? How does realizing our original home enable us to be better servants to all beings? How does the bodhisattva path address these painful inequities of wealth, privilege, and justice? Part of the context for addressing these questions is understanding that those who are born into wealth may not know that their wealth depends on the poverty of others or that their feelings of safety are related to others feeling unsafe.

Many people may want clear and definitive answers to these questions and may feel frustrated when they don't get those answers. Reaching for complete answers is a form of grasping. And definitive answers may trap us into premature understandings. Answers will spontaneously emerge from the bottomless depths of questioning. Without seeking anything, the treasure store will open of itself. We will discover and learn to bring the great resources of compassion and wisdom to the world in which we find ourselves. Right now, we might feel ourselves to be in darkness. We are encouraged by the ancient buddhas to generously, carefully, and patiently feel our way through the darkness to an appropriate response that we do not yet see. I pray that we may continue in our exploration in the midst of our great questions.

We are challenged to address these issues thoroughly and compassionately. Doing so is often uncomfortable, disquieting, and even frightening. As bodhisattvas, we feel a profound wish to be of service in this world of suffering, and yet we might be afraid to embrace it. We may wish to awaken to the truth to promote peace and harmony. This is the aspiration of bodhisattvas in general, and of the Zen tradition in particular.

We started by saying that the buddhas teach that everyone is fully endowed with the wisdom and virtues to help all living beings. The *Avatamsaka Sutra* tells us that all living beings are wealthy and fully possess the best of all things, the wisdom and virtues of the buddhas. Buddhas and bodhisattvas, like the father in the parable, are beings rich in compassion who want to give all their wealth to sentient beings. The *Lotus Sutra* parable reminds us that many sentient beings do not feel and cannot accept that they fully possess the wisdom and virtues of the buddhas.

In Zen we are told that the path of awakening is perfect and all pervading. If so, why is it necessary to train and practice to realize this? There are many ancient examples that explore this profound question. Here is one of them, offered to us by our great compassionate ancestor Eihei Dogen, the founder of Soto Zen in Japan.[3]

> *Zen master Baoche of Mount Mayu was fanning himself. A monk approached and said, "Master, the nature of wind is permanent and there is no place it does not reach. Why, then, do you fan yourself?"*
>
> *"Although you understand that the nature of wind is permanent," Baoche replied, "you do not understand the meaning of its reaching everywhere."*
>
> *"What is the meaning of its reaching everywhere?" asked the monk again.*
>
> *The master just kept fanning himself. The monk bowed deeply.*[4]

All beings are living together in a sea of suffering, and the buddhas are sitting at the center of it all. We have abundant resources to sit with the buddhas and meet and liberate suffering. We are here to help each other discover and actualize the liberating resources of our original home. I want and wish this teaching to be an inspiration, and I pray that it will provide encouragement and guidance for those who wish to address and heal the inequalities and injustices of our whole world.

Now let's consider the myriad forms of fanning the all-pervading wind.

1

The Blooming of the *Lotus Sutra* in Zen Training

IN THE PARABLE OF THE DESTITUTE CHILD, the child's original home is a metaphor for the wondrous dharma of the buddhas. Truly awakened beings of the past and present discovered and realized our original home. This may also be called our buddha-nature, our original face. Our wondrous, inconceivable home is the way we are living in reciprocal dependence together with all beings in the entire universe. Our original home is not a place. Our true being, the way we are really living, isn't confined to existence or nonexistence. It is a middle way, free of both these extremes. It is a relationship in which we are supported by the whole works and in which we support the whole works. We are masterpieces of innumerable stars, and they are masterpieces of us.

It makes sense to many people that we are interdependent with the whole universe. However, they have trouble understanding that this is mutually supportive: They support the whole universe, and the whole universe supports them. My response is that the way we are interdependent with the entire universe, and the way the entire universe is interdependent with us, is not something we can perceive. The way the whole universe supports you and me, and the way you and I support the universe, is imperceptible. It is a process of imperceptible mutual support and assistance.

The Buddha described our original home as "dependent co-arising." We are all dependent co-arisings. Human beings, trees, mountains, rivers, and the great earth are dependent co-arisings. We are born, we live, and we die in the midst of an inconceivable and imperceptible process of dependent co-arising. Not only do other things give us birth; we also give birth to all other things. Our original home is *co*-production. We are not self-produced; we are other-produced. And others are not self-produced; they also are other-produced, and we are part of the other that produces all beings. Each of us is a self, a unique self, a unique person, and each of us is a coproduction of imperceptible, boundless causes and conditions. The whole universe is producing individual things, and individual things are producing the whole universe.

All beings are calling and listening. We are all calling for compassion, and we are also being called to be compassionate. This calling and being called is constant and imperceptible. We are being called to become buddhas.

Just being ourselves, without moving, in stillness and in silence, we are in conversation with all beings. This conversation in silence is what we are, right now. And now. And now. The way the universe creates us to be in each moment is immovable. Because of the way we are made by the whole universe, we are impermanent and constantly changing. We are in an unlimited, continuous conversation with all beings, as they are with us. The way we are, together with all beings, includes all feelings and perceptions and is beyond them. This is our original home, our original nature. This is what Zen meditation is all about.

Living beings are born with a deluded consciousness that has an innate tendency and desire to grasp objects. Because of this, when we are born, we are not able to face and embrace our wondrous, ungraspable, original home. Instead, to exercise and satisfy our grasping tendencies, we are given the ability to project a perceptual enclosure upon our original home. Our minds superimpose perceptions upon the imperceptible process of dependent co-arising, which is our original home. But dependent co-arising cannot be reached by such projections. By virtue of this projecting and grasping, we separate ourselves from the basic matrix of our life. Because of this separation, we often fear intimations of our ungraspable home, and we fear being alone. At the same time, we deeply long for reunion with what we fear. We long for reunion with that which we have never really left. Thus, we begin a long journey of recovering and realizing our original home.

Our original home, our original nature, is ever-present, inconceivable, and ungraspable. However, our deluded mind, in its habitual tendency to grasp, creates a graspable version of the ungraspable. Without thorough study of this mind, we tend to strongly adhere to its projections as being the way things actually are. When we adhere to these projections on reality, we become alienated from our wondrous true home. In the midst of this alienation, we yearn for our original home and hunger to return to it. Motivated by this profound hunger to return to our original home, we imagine we need to go away from where we already are to find it. This is a misconception. We are like the child in the *Lotus Sutra*.

When they feel separated, children need compassion to help them deal with the frightening sense of separation. We too might imagine that we have been abandoned or that we could be abandoned, and we also may feel terrified at those times. What we need to learn is how to practice compassion with the terror that arises in such imaginings.

For example, when I was two years old, I contracted polio and became a patient at the Sister Kenny Institute in Minneapolis. As was the custom in hospitals at that time, my parents were not allowed to stay there with me. Although I was probably frightened by being separated from them, there was kindness all around me teaching me how to deal with my fear. I had an implicit sense that I was being cared for very deeply and widely. I have memories of dark rooms and hallways with people in white clothing caring for me and saying, "You're such a good boy, a good boy." They had to stretch, massage, and exercise my paralyzed arms and legs so that they would not atrophy. This was groundbreaking treatment but was also painful, and those kind people helped me get through it.

When I went home from the Sister Kenny Institute, my mother continued to help me do those painful stretching exercises. She could see it was painful for me, and she cried for me. We continued these exercises for years. Perhaps because of the kindness and support I received, a confidence began to grow in me about the great potential of working compassionately with physical and mental pain in myself and others.

The way I experienced my situation was that I was painfully separated from my parents, but I also perceived that I was being cared for. One perception was painful, and the other was soothing. Becoming free of painful perceptions of separation or abandonment requires learning how to be kind toward those painful experiences. In the parable of the destitute child, we see his pain and his fear, and we see him being taught how to be compassionate toward them by his father's kindness and respect.

We need new stories to free us from our old stories. The *Lotus Sutra* parable provides a path to becoming free of all our stories and awakening to our original home beyond all our stories. As our compassionate patience for our horror stories of not being supported matures, we come to trust and understand that we are always supported by others, and we are always supporting them. By practicing compassion for the pain of our stories, we will come to a place where we dare to face and open up to our original home.

However, before our compassion has matured, we are still at risk of being confused. For example, instead of being compassionate to our painful stories with a sense of being embraced and sustained, we become involved in various activities to control and vouchsafe support. Ironically, those activities implicitly and explicitly deny that we are supported. We imagine that we have to do something to be loved and supported. We imagine that certain things are necessary to receive support, such as cleaning our room, being quiet at the dinner table, agreeing with our parents or our children, doing well in school, getting a good job, and so on. We may imagine that if we don't do these things, we won't receive support. And sadly, even our friends and family may sometimes seem to support this view. Sometimes people say, "If you want support, you've got to do this," rather than "You're already loved no matter what you do, and I want you to do this."

In our original home we are supported by others and, at the same time, we support them. All-pervading mutual support *is* our original home. Whether we clean our room or not, whether we are "good" children or not, we always are supported and supportive. But our original home also allows us to imagine that we're not supported, and it allows us to imagine that we have to do something to get supported.

Many of us have stories about how we will be supported and stories about how we are supported. In the Zen tradition, we also have stories about how to practice so that we can fully appreciate the reality of mutual support beyond all of our stories. Through our training, we learn to be mindful of the teaching that our perceptions are not what our life really is. Also, we are taught not to push our perceptions away but rather to learn to be compassionate toward all of them. The story I just told you points us toward our original home where you and I are supported no matter what we do, and no matter what we do, we support the whole universe.

Our original home is where we are actually and inconceivably giving and receiving in concert with the entire universe. This giving and receiving is simultaneous, mutual, and reciprocal. Within ordinary consciousness, this mutual support is perceived as coming and going, but fundamentally it is unceasing and imperceptible. The way that we are actually mutually embraced and sustained together with all beings is beyond our hearing, seeing, feeling, and imagining. It is through our ordinary, conceivable practice that we touch and realize the inconceivable truth of the thoroughgoing mutual support of our original home. And yet within the perceptions of deluded consciousness, it might seem to us that this mutual support appears and disappears, that it comes and goes. However, this fundamental, inconceivable mutual support is the way things actually are.

Some might ask how we can know a truth that is beyond our perceptions. The parable of the destitute child speaks directly to this question. At the beginning, the son does not perceive or understand this mutual support. However, by the end of the parable, after going through the process of training in the stables and in the house, the actual inconceivable, imperceptible reality of this mutual support is fully realized. The name of the chapter in which the parable appears is called "Faith and Understanding." By faithfully engaging in all the ordinary, perceptible practices that are given to him, shoveling dung in the stables and working in the business of the great house, the son awakens and understands his original home. This is about the relationship between concrete practice and absolute truth. This relationship is extremely deep, and by "deep" I mean difficult to understand. We have just attempted to clarify this relationship, but even after clarification it remains ambiguous.

It is crucial to give up the slightest discrepancy between the practice, the training, and realization of the truth. If there is a hairbreadth difference between them, we fail to accord with the proper attunement.[1]

Whether we know it or not, we ask the universe for support, and it supports us in response. It also asks us for support, and we respond in kind whether we know it or not. This message has been transmitted by ancient teachers who have realized it. It may be hard to believe and hard to understand this, even though it is reality. We need a training program to realize this teaching. Then we will be free, totally free, to teach all beings how to awaken to this reality.

Buddhas and ancestors invite and encourage us to be compassionate to our stories of support and nonsupport. In this way, our stories are opportunities to return to our original nature, which has never been separate from us.

When we or others are frightened, we often tell soothing stories to help ourselves or others to calm down. For example, a child might become aware that people die and wonder if their own mother will die and become terrified about that possibility. This child might ask their mother if she's going to die, and their mother might say soothingly, "Oh, I'm not going to die for a really long time." The soothing stories we tell ourselves might be necessary until we are able to observe our frightening and unhappy stories with compassion. The soothing stories might be appropriate tranquilizers for the pain of our disturbing stories. However, we need to be careful with these stories lest we become addicted to them.

Once upon a time, a monk asked the great teacher Mazu,[2] "I heard you teach that mind itself is buddha. Is that so?" Mazu replied, "I teach that to help children stop crying." Then the monk asked, "What do you teach after they stop crying?" And Mazu said, "No mind, no buddha."[3]

Calming and encouraging stories are expedient means that we might need to use until we can accept and practice the real teaching. If we are compassionate toward our fears and feelings of alienation, we no longer have to tell ourselves stories to cope with them. On the path of great awakening, feelings and frightening stories do arise. When we practice compassion toward all stories, we see that all along those stories have been calling us to practice compassion, and we understand that compassion has always been our original nature. Then we can transmit this compassion and realization to others. As the *Lotus Sutra* teaches, this great compassion is our original home.

2

The Path of Buddha

OUR ORIGINAL NATURE IS ALWAYS PRESENT, but without guidance and training we don't understand this to be true, and so we yearn for it. Our original nature is the truth of what we really are, but in our confusion, we wander away into destitution and yearn to find it again. Sometimes the yearning is subtle and vague. It may be a mysterious feeling. Sometimes it may be tormenting. In our foolish search for that which we never lost, we will eventually reencounter it. However, as we mentioned earlier, in the initial encounter, we might not be ready to accept it.

In this state of unreadiness, the teachings tell us that someday we will be kindly offered skillful guidance, and our faith and understanding will grow. Inevitably we will receive and actualize our original nature and transmit this actualization to others. This is the reality of our life. Within this process, we realize and practice the nonduality of guidance and being guided. In our family, this nondual practice is nicknamed Zen.

Like other families, the Zen family goes through difficult and stressful times. All families are held together by good stories. For the purpose of holding the family together, we have various collections of sustaining stories. One of the collections is called the *Book of Serenity*. These one hundred stories were gathered together by the great Song dynasty teacher Hongzhi,[1] who also wrote verse commentaries on each story. These stories show the playfulness of the Zen family. This collection in particular shows that ultimate truth (principle) and conventional truths (phenomena) are interfused and dynamically pivot on each other. Although these stories play a vital role in the maintenance of the Zen family, they are far too important to be taken seriously.

Case 56 in the *Book of Serenity* is called "Uncle Mi and the White Rabbit."[2] It is a conversation between our ancestor Dongshan Liangjie[3] and his elder dharma brother Sengmi, whom we affectionately call Uncle Mi.

> *As Dongshan and his spiritual uncle, Mi, were walking along, a white rabbit ran by in front of them. Mi said, "Swift!"*
>
> *Dongshan said, "How?"*
>
> *Mi said, "Like a commoner being made a prime minister."*
>
> *Dongshan said, "Such a venerable old person still says such words!"*
>
> *Mi said, "Then what about you?"*
>
> *Dongshan said, "Generations of nobility temporarily fallen into poverty."*[4]

These close friends offer us two different ways of looking at the bodhisattva path. One way is that one might go swiftly from being a commoner, an ordinary illiterate person, to being the erudite prime minister of China. In other words, we can quickly go from being an ordinary, deluded, unenlightened living being to becoming a greatly awakened one. The other view is that after generations of innate nobility, we have temporarily fallen into poverty. That is to say, after being born into the family of awakening, one has temporarily fallen into delusion.

It is taught in the Great Vehicle that it takes a very long time to go from being an ordinary, deluded person to being a fully awakened one, so Uncle Mi's way might sound like really good news. He is saying that it need not take so long and that we can go swiftly from being a deluded person to being someone who is enlightened beyond all measures.

In China, for millennia, there were officials and ministers who advised the emperor and helped govern the empire. But before they became officials, these people went through a long and rigorous process of education and training. The Chinese imperial government system was a meritocracy and had various levels of examination for ministers and officials. If those who aspired to become government officials and ministers passed one level of exam, they could go to the next level and so on.

Usually, people who became ministers were born into a family of aristocrats who were educated people. They were educated within the family, and then they went through various steps and stages of increasing skill and erudition. They could learn the sacred texts of the tradition, and they could learn the various skills of calligraphy, music, poetry, horseback riding, and so on; but with rare exceptions, people did not go from being a commoner to being a prime minister. If they did, they never went quickly. However, it was possible for commoners, if they really applied themselves for a long time, to become highly educated persons, great ministers in the vast empire.

In the story about Uncle Mi and Dongshan, Uncle Mi offers us the extraordinary possibility of rapidly going through what is usually a very long process of going from being an illiterate commoner to becoming a learned prime minister. He said, “It’s like a commoner quickly being made a prime minister.”

Uncle Mi knew that the usual way of going from being ordinary to being extraordinary, or from being a commoner to being a sage, is a long and arduous one involving various methods of cultivation. This is the view of gradual awakening by skillful means. But when Uncle Mi sees the white rabbit rapidly crossing the road, he holds up the attractive possibility that the process of cultivation could be swift.

Dongshan’s view is that we are originally endowed with the wisdom and virtues of a great sage. He says to his elder, “Hmm, such a venerable person and you still talk like that.” Then Uncle Mi says, “How about you?” and Dongshan says, “After generations of nobility temporarily fallen into poverty.” Like Uncle Mi, we might imagine our path as a journey from being an ordinary person to becoming an extraordinary sage by working on ourselves using various provisional means. For example, in the parable of the destitute child, the son works on himself by shoveling dung in the stables. Through the use of such means, we apply ourselves in our ordinary lives and see ourselves moving forward through various stages of training. In this vision of practice there appears to be an opportunity to use human agency to improve ourselves. It seems that we can do something through our personal effort to become someone other than who we already are. Dongshan emphatically cautioned Uncle Mi about this point of view.

The rabbit crossing the road is a metaphor for going from ordinary to extraordinary. In our ordinary way of thinking, we are often involved in trying to do something. When we hear about awakening and wish to realize it, we imagine that we will awaken to something other than who we truly are. Then we might think, "What can I do to become an awakened person?" We might want someone to tell us a story about how we can become buddha.

The *Lotus Sutra* tells us that we are bodhisattvas and that we will become buddhas. The parable of the destitute child tells us that buddhahood is our original home and true nature. This vision of the bodhisattva path starts from the true nature of awakening and enters into the ordinariness of delusion. From Dongshan's point of view, this is our actual situation. He says we start with great wisdom and compassion that is in intimate communion with all beings, but we have temporarily forgotten it. Great wisdom and compassion need to wholeheartedly and temporarily enter into ordinariness in order to free all beings so they may live in peace. The parable tells us that our innate awakening needs to enter into ordinariness to realize itself.

In this version of the story, we don't have to do anything special to become buddha. We just have to be completely ourselves. Why is that? Because for a sentient being to just be a sentient being is precisely awakening. The only way we can be completely ourselves is by working for the welfare of all beings. We are already at the seat of awakening, but we have a strong tendency to think that we need to do something in order to be where we already are. Isn't this ironic?

Dongshan tells us that after generations of wholeheartedly practicing the buddha way, we have temporarily fallen into the poverty of trying to get somewhere. Uncle Mi's view is that of poverty; the view that wishes to get somewhere quickly. From that point of view, he is happy to announce that it's possible to get somewhere swiftly, but the *Lotus Sutra* says this has nothing to do with being swift. This is faster than swift. It is not about going any place. It is about what we are and have been all along. We already are offspring of awakening. We are already engaged in buddhas' work in the house of the buddhas.

We fully possess the great wisdom and virtues of awakening, but because of the bodhisattva vow, we go beyond awakening and enter into the poverty of ordinary life for the welfare of living beings.

And what is the bodhisattva vow? There are innumerable ways of expressing this. One way is called the four universal vows expressed by the following *gatha*:

Sentient beings are numberless; we vow to save them.
Afflictions are inexhaustible; we vow to cut through.
Dharma gates are boundless; we vow to enter them.
Buddha way is unsurpassable; we vow to become it.

A simpler form of the bodhisattva vow is to commit to realizing authentic awakening for the welfare of the world.

The entry into ordinariness from what we truly are is not done merely by human agency. It is accomplished by the power of the bodhisattva vow whether we know it or not. The vow lets go of our original reality and responds to all living beings by knowingly and willingly plunging into ordinary life. "Ordinariness" is not different from what we truly are, and wandering away from it is not different from it either. Compassionately entering into ordinariness realizes our original nature for the welfare of the world. Our ordinariness includes all beings and is included in all beings.

Uncle Mi's way of practicing is to go from being ordinary to being a sage by means of cultivation, by means of human agency and doing this swiftly. This is the commoner quickly becoming a prime minister. Dongshan's way is to realize the nonduality of sagehood and ordinariness by the power of vow, free of all human agency. In our original nature, there is a deep vow to realize buddhahood by harmonizing sagehood and ordinariness.

Some might wonder where this vow comes from. The vow doesn't come from buddha, and it doesn't come from sentient beings. The vow comes from the inconceivably intimate communion of buddhas and sentient beings. This call and response between buddhas and sentient beings is our original nature. This communion is shining brightly in the darkness even as we wander.

Dongshan is telling us about our original nature, that we are all children in the family of the buddhas and bodhisattvas. We are bodhisattvas, and we have only temporarily fallen into the poverty of forgetfulness and distraction by the power of the vow. Dongshan and the *Lotus Sutra* tell us we have been bodhisattvas for generations, and we have temporarily forgotten that. Even though the buddha way is our original nature, without training we do not really understand that. Ironically, it is our nature that we need to practice to know what we really are. And paradoxically, part of realizing our nature is to wander away from it.

As the parable in the *Lotus Sutra* says, part of the path of returning to and realizing our true nature may involve working through feelings of inferiority and worthlessness. This is Uncle Mi's version of awakening. Thus, we humbly enter into training, like the son entered into shoveling dung. Realizing and awakening to our original nature, we become free of ordinary and extraordinary.

When we accept and realize what we truly are, we need not look for it anymore. We awaken to who we really are, have always been, and always will be. We understand what our family is, wholeheartedly care for it, and transmit it to future generations.

We come from boundless abundance and yet, as bodhisattvas, we must enter into the limitations of poverty in order to develop the skills we need to fulfill our original nature and benefit all beings. The intimate business of the buddhas must work equally with poverty and wealth to manifest itself. In this realization we see that our poverty and our wealth are inseparable.

In the Tang dynasty there was a monk who seemed to have heard the teaching that all sentient beings are endowed with the wisdom and virtues of the buddhas. He seems, unlike many of us, to have had a low opinion of dogs and wondered how this teaching applied to them, so he went to meet with the great teacher Zhaozhou.[5]

A monk asked Zhaozhou, "Does a dog have buddha-nature?"

Zhaozhou said, "It has."

Then the monk asked, "Since it has, why has it entered this skin bag?"

Zhaozhou said, "Because it knowingly and willingly transgresses."[6]

Our original nature, which embraces the unlimited bodhisattva vow, knowingly and willingly transgresses into any limitation, including poverty and wealth, that might be of benefit to beings.

Alluding to the *Lotus Sutra*, Dongshan taught us that we have been living in abundance on and off for generations and have now temporarily fallen into poverty. The *Flower Adornment Scripture* tradition also teaches this.

As we said earlier, in that scripture, the Buddha taught that we are all fully endowed with the wisdom and virtues of the buddhas, but because of attachments and misconceptions, we do not understand this. Buddha is like the father in the parable. Buddhas are beings of abundant compassion and skill who want to give all their wealth to sentient beings. Bodhisattvas are like the child who wandered away from his original nature into destitution.

Our true nature is not sagehood or ordinariness, wealth or poverty. What we really are is the harmony of sagehood and ordinariness, the nonduality of poverty and abundance. Realizing this nonduality, we leap beyond both of them and actualize our true nature. This is an interpretation of the *Lotus Sutra* parable as expressed through the story of Dongshan and Uncle Mi. Bodhisattvas let go of wealth and enter into poverty to help people. They do so in order to actualize their true nature rather than trying to escape poverty and enter into wealth.

3

Wandering Away

OUR ORIGINAL NATURE IS THE LIFE OF IMPERCEPTIBLE, intimate, mutual communion among all beings. However, because human beings are deeply conditioned to try to grasp things, our body and mind give rise to perceptible versions of our ungraspable original nature. These illusory perceptible versions are incoherent and confused, and they obscure what we really are. They cover our view of the whole world. The reality of our life is inconceivable and ungraspable. But when we grasp a perceptible version of it, we suffer and yearn for the reality of our original nature. Our original nature is our intimacy with beings. Because of this, we mistakenly feel, knowingly or unknowingly, that we must wander away from where we are right now to find what we are yearning for.

For some people, the home they know is quite loving, supportive, and wholesome. They see their parents and other family members as being kind to them, loving them, and being willing and able to nurture them. Seeing this, they are grateful.

Sadly, other people suffer in the midst of more painful perceptions of their home. They may think that their home is not blessed, that they are not fortunate, that their family members don't love them, that they are unskillful and even abusive, or that they are impoverished and unable to help them.

However, no matter how we perceive our home and family, we still yearn to realize our wondrous, inconceivable, original nature. In Zen, we call this home our original face before our parents were born.

Thus, I have heard. Shakyamuni Buddha had loving parents who wished to protect him from all harm, from seeing and feeling all forms of suffering. Still, one day he left his home and saw the inevitable suffering of the world. In this vision, he saw that something was missing in his understanding of life. Eventually, he left the palace to search for his true home, which he did not yet understand. It took him a long time to realize who he truly is. He found that out by becoming aware of his own suffering.

In the *Lotus Sutra*, when the destitute, downtrodden son reencountered his father after long and oblivious wandering, the son did not recognize his father and could not take in the reality that this was actually his home. The son was awestruck by his first glimpse of his father's home and tried to run away.

This is the process that we are also in. It is the process of realizing our original nature in the midst of our alienation from it. We're on the same journey as the Buddha, and we have parents, families, friends, and teachers to help us walk this path.

No matter how we perceive our nature, any nature that we are able to see is not our original nature; and yet our original nature is never apart from our perceptions. Because we don't know that our original nature is always with us, we wander away searching for it. All beings wander off from their visible home to find peace by rediscovering and realizing who they really are—even though that has never even been a hairbreadth away from wherever they are right now. We only think it is separate from where we are, and therefore we feel driven to go someplace in search of it. Furthermore, we think we strike out on this journey on our own. We think we set up the parameters of our great experiment by ourselves. In walking this path, we might even want to be free of dependence on our parents and teachers. In order to find our own path, we might feel a need to reject the values that our home and family transmitted to us.

In the parable of the destitute child, it does not say that this young person was a teenager when he wandered away, but I imagine him to be so. It's not only teenagers who are afflicted by the desire to be anywhere other than where they are, but perhaps this desire to be somewhere else is most powerful when we are adolescents. There is a deep and reoccurring wish to escape and to be free of adult supervision, scrutiny, and possible interference. In the midst of their hormonal storms, they want privacy. This can be seen in terms of biological evolution for the purposes of reproduction, and it can also be seen in terms of spiritual evolution for the purpose of awakening. It's not really that we go away to escape our parents but that we go away to understand who we really are.

In my life, I felt loved and supported by my parents; however, they separated from each other when I was about eleven years old. This offered me opportunities to escape parental supervision and experiment with wandering away from home. Part of me was sad about the separation and part of me was glad that my father went away because I felt free to do things that I wouldn't have been able to do with him still living in our house. I thought that I had an opportunity to break away from my father, my mother, my teachers, and from the whole system of support and expectations I had known. After all, my father had given me the nickname "Reb."

My father's leaving our home gave me space and opportunity to try dangerous and rebellious things that I don't think I would have attempted or dared to do with him in the house and to learn that they were mistakes. I didn't think about it at the time, but these adventures may also have been partially expressing the anger I felt toward my father for leaving our family.

At that time in my life, the lost and rebellious spirits that James Dean and Marlon Brando played in their films really attracted me. Even when I was only twelve years old, I really identified with them. They played confused young men who were searching for something that they, and I, vaguely sensed. In their portrayal of these lost and searching beings, they radiated a great light. The radiance of their performances touched me deeply. In my adolescent mind, it occurred to me that if I copied their wild and dangerous behavior, I would be beautiful too. I was unaware of the impermanence of my youth, vitality, and health. My adolescent sense of indestructibility intoxicated me and, being intoxicated, I thought I could act with impunity.

One night one of my friends, a boy who was about a year older than me, had the brilliant idea to take a car from an auto repair garage and go for a joyride. I had never driven a car, but my friend had a little driving experience. Somehow we got into the garage, found the keys to the cars that were parked outside, took one set of those keys, found the car, started it up, and drove away. As I remember, it was a 1950 Hudson sedan.

We were driving around Minneapolis in the middle of the night, having lots of fun. We were also having various difficulties because my friend didn't know how to drive well. The car had a stick shift, and often in the process of his unskillful shifting, the car would stall out. He also sometimes had trouble turning corners. Near the conclusion of our ride, we came around a corner a little too fast, and I slid from the passenger's side of the front seat over into the driver's side. I bumped into my friend, and he lost control of the car. Instead of turning the corner, we ran into a tree by Lake Harriet. My friend wasn't hurt, but my wrist was sprained. We ran away from the car.

This happened around sunrise so almost no one was around, but a man who was fishing saw us running away. Maybe he was the one who called the police because after some time, we saw a police car coming. We tried to run away and hide behind some cars, but they found us easily. After they took us to the hospital for my wrist to be treated, they took us to jail and fingerprinted and booked us, just like in the movies. It was kind of enjoyable for me at the time, to go to jail at twelve years old. In my middle-class neighborhood, kids almost never went to jail, so this was very exciting, like James Dean going to jail in *Rebel Without a Cause*.

As we were being taken to our cells, we walked by a cell that was full of colorfully dressed young women. When they saw a twelve- and a thirteen-year-old boy being brought in, they got quite lively, and they reached through the bars to us. It was very exciting, having these so-called ladies of the night reaching out to us. But when my mother came to spring us from jail, there was so much embarrassment and anger in her face that it stopped being fun, and I felt really ashamed that I had done something that was so painful for her. She was very unhappy about the whole situation. I had a leather jacket and motorcycle boots that she took away.

In my intoxication I didn't think about how terrible it would be for my mother to have to pick me up from jail, but it was terrible, and I was really regretful and ashamed that I had hurt her. Perhaps this regret primed me to be open to some good advice, which I received afterward. I survived this delinquent activity relatively unscathed, but many people don't.

After this wild night and the next morning in jail, we went to school in the afternoon. I told my partner in crime, "Let's not tell people at school what happened," but he did. That night there was a dance near our school, and a lot of our classmates and friends were there. I went to the dance and, since my friend had told people about our run-in with the law, many of them treated us as if we were heroes. Doing something like that was very unusual in our neighborhood and, for some of our friends, it sounded bold, exciting, and adventurous. Coming into the room where the dance was being held, lots of people responded in a celebratory way. It was almost like a ticker-tape parade.

There was a policeman at the dance for security. Somebody told him about what I had done, and I wound up talking to him about it. He seemed accepting of it and nonjudgmental. I even remember him saying something like "the wilder the colt, the better the horse." In some sense, it seemed that wild adventures were not that bad, although I did really regret how disturbing it was to my mother's mind and heart. Although I didn't feel inhibited from a path of further adventures in juvenile delinquency, I did in fact retire from them. I could see that such a path was not that cool, and I never took any other cars for joyrides.

I was really fortunate. The formal charge was taking a car without permission, and my punishment was not that severe, but I was on probation for a year and had to check in with a probation officer once a month. When I did, I saw other boys and girls from many different backgrounds in the waiting room with me. I don't know what road they took after probation, but my partner in this adventure went on from taking a car without permission to taking cars and selling them, which is called grand theft auto. He was eventually sent to reform school until he was eighteen.

Fortunately, I was given help and support to see that this path I was on was a dead end. Unfortunately, not all teenagers are in circumstances where they are lovingly helped and supported to look at what they did and perhaps to see that this was not the kind of life they would really wish to live.

In the apartment building where my mother, sister, brother, and I lived, there was a man who had two daughters but no son. He was always kind and friendly to me. He loved his daughters, but I think he also wanted a son. After my father left, he took a more active interest in me, and he became a mentor and good father figure, maybe due to my mother's encouragement. His name was Dick Grant. He was about forty at that time, but when he was in his twenties, he had been a heavyweight Golden Gloves champion boxer. He was a big guy, six feet four inches tall and 240 pounds. I weighed 140 then and was playing football. He invited me to get down face-to-face with him, like two football linemen facing each other. Then he jumped at me, and I had the opportunity to try to block him. Having this giant lunge at me was rather scary, but I appreciated the opportunity.

When he heard about my delinquent behavior, he came to talk to me. He told me about his childhood and some of his wild adventures. I was impressed. He was as daring as I was. He wasn't trying to show me that he was better than me, but he did let me know that he'd tried experiments similar to what I was doing. Then he told me something I'll never forget. He said, "You know, it's easy to be bad. What's hard is to be good." I immediately thought, "That's true. Okay, I think I'll do what's hard; I'll try to be good."

Although I had that thought, I still didn't know how to go about being good, but I found his words to be really intriguing and encouraging. He was like one of the workers in the *Lotus Sutra* parable that the father sent to offer the son a job in the stables. He was someone I could relate to, and he offered me a job opportunity that I found attractive. I could accept it just as the son could gladly accept the job of working in the stables shoveling dung. If my school principal, who represented the law and order of the school, had made that same statement without disclosing his childhood errors, I wouldn't have been so interested.

My father also came to me to talk about the car incident. We met at another lake in Minneapolis and took a walk around it. Then we sat down and talked about what happened. Rather than telling me that I was a bad boy and that I should stop, and possibly implying that he was better than me, he said that he had similar problems when he was young. Just as Dick Grant had done, my father told me how he'd gotten into trouble with the law when he was in college. My father also asked me to remember how hard it would be for my mother if I continued to do things like joyriding. He didn't say it would be hard for him, but he did say that it would be hard for my mother.

Instead of approaching me from a position of moral superiority, both of these men said, "I was like you." In both cases, I really felt supported and encouraged to be more aware of what I was doing and the consequences of my actions. Those conversations helped me to find another path rather than continuing on such an exciting, inconsiderate, and thoughtless path.

Our parents, family, and teachers often show us how to pay attention to our actions. Going off from home to do fun things often starts before we actually leave the home of our parents. The human nervous system is geared to do things that appear to be fun, but at the same time there is also often a subtle and deeper wish to realize our true nature.

One Sunday afternoon, when I was around thirteen years old, I was feeling sad and at a loss about my life. I was at home in my own room, and an insight arose that all the painful problems I had in my life would drop away if I just focused on being kind to others rather than being concerned with my own popularity and standing among my friends and schoolmates. It struck me that that would be really good. This insight stayed with me, and I felt good about this new approach to my life: Do what's good; be kind to people.

I remember going to school the next morning with the intention of focusing on being kind to people. Then I opened the door, went into the crowded hallway, and saw all these lovely young people, particularly the girls, and I forgot about my intention. My mind switched from the intention of being kind to others to my usual mode of being concerned about how others felt about me and whether they liked me or not. I had a glimmer of wanting to do what was good, but it was really hard to remember to do it. My intention got washed away in the flood of hormones and exciting self-concern of teenage life. But I still had some awareness of wanting to do good and a growing sense that I needed some kind of training in order to do so.

Generally speaking, the longer we wander on our own, searching for the reality of who we are, the more destitute and impoverished we become. In reality, we can't leave what we are because it is not separate from where we are right now. But we can experience the impoverishing consequences of implicitly and explicitly denying it by going away from where we are right now in search of it.

At some point we need training in how to skillfully observe our impulses to do things we think would be pleasureful or fun. Many people have found their way to Zen practice in the process of recovering from seeking peace and happiness through substances and addictive behaviors. Addictions are, fundamentally, wandering away from where we are. As we wander through the destitution and desperation of addictively seeking fulfillment, we eventually will come to see, more or less clearly, that we need to receive training in recovery from our addictions. The forms of this training may also help us to see that we need further training to understand something beyond recovery in order to realize our true nature. This recovery process helps us do the work of realizing the ultimate and profound concerns of our life.

I would like to respectfully acknowledge that the forms in which this process of wandering and alienation manifests are not the same for all people. The forms of wandering are unlimited.

One woman told me the way she wandered away was by becoming pregnant. Another woman told me that she wandered away by marrying someone her parents disliked. There is an old Chinese legend from the Tang dynasty about a woman named Senjo. Reverend Eijun Linda Ruth Cutts tells the story as follows:

> *Senjo was the beloved daughter of Chokan. In childhood she played with her cousin Ochu, and Senjo's father jokingly told them they were betrothed. They believed him and later fell in love. When her father told her she should marry another man, they were heartbroken.*
>
> *Ochu left the village in a boat before the marriage. As he left, he saw a figure running along the riverbank, calling to him. It was Senjo. Joyfully she joined him, and they traveled far away, where they married and had two children.*
>
> *Five years went by and Senjo longed to see her parents and ask their forgiveness. They traveled back to their village, and Ochu went to her father, told him the story, and apologized for them both.*
>
> *Chokan, astonished, asked Ochu, "What girl are you talking about?"*

"Your daughter Senjo," replied Ochu.

Chokan said, "My daughter Senjo? Ever since you left, she's been sick in bed, unable to speak."

Then Ochu brought Senjo up from the boat. As they approached her parents' door, the Senjo who had been sick got up from her bed, smiling. When the two Senjos met, they merged into one.

Senjo said, "I saw Ochu going away and that night I dreamed that I ran after his boat. But now I cannot tell which was really me—the one that went away in the boat or the one that stayed at home."

Later Zen Master Wuzu asked, "Senjo was separated from her soul. Which was the real Senjo?"[1]

In commenting on this story, Reverend Eijun said, "The conventional elements of the story mirror many of the situations that brought me and many women to practice. Like Senjo we may have grown up in circumstances in which we had little agency, where familial, religious, cultural, gender and social pressures were strong and where meeting the prevailing expectations was conveyed as more important than anything else. . . . We may try to relieve our pain in unskillful ways. . . . Eventually we begin longing to be whole—for something real, for our true home."[2]

Suzuki Roshi's son, Hoitsu Suzuki Roshi, told us a story about when he was a young priest in college. He said that he went to college to study Buddhism, but in fact he was mostly interested in training in kendo, the Japanese art of dueling with swords. This is the way a young Japanese priest searched for his own way. Even so, he was interested enough in Buddhism to sincerely ask his father, his teacher, "What is Buddhism?" His father simply replied, "Harmony."

Thus, they realized the harmony of the student's call and the teacher's response together. Because the student was wholeheartedly training in kendo, he was open to receiving the buddhas' subtle transmission of call-and-response. When we understand this subtle teaching, we too will be in peace and harmony with all beings.

My wandering continued when I left my family home and went to study at the University of Minnesota. I was consciously aware that I was looking for my life's work, my occupation, my profession. I had gone to school, I had done many kinds of manual labor from childhood through my teens, and I understood that I was looking for something else. In high school, I wasn't searching for my life's work through my academic studies or my sports career. But when I went to university, I was. I didn't know what I was looking for, but I thought that in the process of studying, I might discover what my life's work would be. During the four years as an undergraduate, first majoring in premed and then in math, and my three years in graduate school studying personality psychology, I was looking for what I wanted to do with this precious life.

During my college years, I read stories about Zen folks, and I thought they were really cool. In these stories, I saw a glimmer of what we really are. While reading them, I saw images of what I was looking for. Those images gave me a glimpse of a truth I was yearning for. One of the stories that gave me a glimpse of the truth was about the Zen Master Hakuin.[3]

Hakuin was praised by his neighbors as one living a pure life.

A beautiful Japanese girl whose parents owned a food store, lived near him. Suddenly without any warning, her parents discovered she was with child.

This made her parents angry. She would not confess who the man was, but after much harassment at last she named Hakuin.

In great anger the parents went to the master. "Is that so?" was all he would say.

After the child was born, it was brought to Hakuin. By this time, he had lost his reputation, which did not trouble him, but he took very good care of the child. He obtained milk from his neighbors and everything else the little one needed.

A year later, the girl-mother could stand it no longer. She told her parents the truth—that the real father of the child was a young man who worked in the fish market.

The mother and father of the girl at once went to Hakuin to ask his forgiveness, to apologize at length, and to get the child back again.

Hakuin was willing. In yielding the child, all he said was "Is that so?"[4]

Reading this I said to myself, "That's how I want to be. I want to be like that." I wanted to become a person like that who responds appropriately, in accord with reality. I thought all the people in the Zen stories I read were really cool, and I wanted to be like them. But then I wondered how does one become like those Zen men, women, and children? It didn't seem like becoming that way came by accident.

As a child, I deeply appreciated the stories I heard about Jesus, and I still do. However, Jesus often was portrayed in ways that seemed inaccessibly different from me. I could relate to his suffering and death, and I thought it was cool that Jesus told people who are criticizing others to look at themselves. I could relate to that teaching. I wanted to learn how to look at myself and give up criticizing others. But I didn't know how to become such a person.

The stories of the Zen people also demonstrated this teaching, but I didn't think they were supernormal, holy people. Although they appeared different from me, the way they were seemed accessible. I was attracted to that way and wanted to learn it.

These people weren't demonstrating a supernormal way of walking; they were simply showing how to walk gently on the earth. They were showing how to open your hands and close your hands appropriately in response to the needs of others. Being able to open our hands appropriately, no matter what, and to be able to close them appropriately, no matter what, looked possible. It looked like freedom. It looked really cool. I wanted to be like that, but how?

When I was at university, I was involved in academic studies to train my mind. After getting my undergraduate degree, having nothing better to do, I went to graduate school. In graduate school, I was given a brilliant, kind advisor. He gradually let me know what it would be like to be fully in training with him and offered to mentor me. He started to show me how to fully engage in his discipline of social science. He was making this offering to someone who was looking for what he really wanted to do in his life. And I was looking at him to see if what he was offering was the life I really wanted. If it was, I would have willingly made the effort—the considerable effort—to do the necessary work.

I brought some Zen teachings that I had been studying into our discussions in his seminars around that time. I had already visited Tassajara Zen Mountain Center the previous summer,[5] and my advisor could see signs that I was moving in that direction. Maybe because of this, he nicknamed me the Swami. Even though my advisor was really open-minded, my experience was that these Buddhist teachings seemed too big to fit into the psychology we were studying. On the other hand, I was beginning to see that the psychology we were studying could fit nicely within the teachings of Buddhism. Maybe in response to that, my advisor was asking me to consider whether I wanted to engage in more thorough training in the field of academic psychology with him.

When I was in high school, I had seen a photograph in *Life* magazine of a silhouetted person sitting upright and cross-legged on a tatami mat. This person was seated in a dark room overlooking a luminous garden. The caption beneath the photograph was "In Deepest Thought."[6] The photograph itself was deeply moving to me, and the caption stimulated an insight. I thought, "Yes, that body posture looks like deepest thought. And deepest thought has a beautiful posture."

That insight planted a seed in me about the intimate relationship between the quality of our bodily posture and the quality of our mind. When we're in deepest thought, our body posture has an inner beauty. I was deeply touched and attracted to this vision of embodied deep thought. Now I would say that the truth of my original nature was revealed to me in the form of this body and mind. Like the destitute child in the *Lotus Sutra*, I was awestruck by this vision; but unlike him, I didn't feel fear in this encounter. I was attracted to it and remembered it, whereas he ran away.

So one day, as I was considering the training my kind advisor was offering to me, I saw him eating at McDonald's. He was a tall man, and he was sitting bent over his hamburger. The shape of his bodily posture formed a kind of a question mark. Although he was a brilliant intellect and a great man, when I saw this, I understood that I didn't want to be his disciple. I thought that I would be trained more deeply if my body was included in the training.

I wanted training that would develop my senses, both mental and physical, to be more aware and receptive of how our world is changing and where it's going intellectually, artistically, and spiritually. I felt that my advisor was encouraging me to amass greater knowledge of academic psychology, but I was more drawn to developing a sense of how psychology and other disciplines were evolving together. I wanted to train myself to develop those senses. I heard from various quarters the suggestion that the Eastern traditions offered psychophysical training for this purpose. My academic advisor generously offered me a wonderful opportunity to train my mind in academic psychology but that wasn't comprehensive enough for me. I wanted training that included my body and the world beyond the institution of the university. I thought that such training would be more complete and truer to the life that I was searching for.

Our original nature is the embodiment of profound thought. I wondered where I could receive the kind of training that would realize such profound thought and beautiful posture. I wanted to train my eyes and ears and nose and tongue and skin and mind. I wanted to see examples of beings who gave up looking elsewhere for the truth of their lives. I wanted to learn from others how to be myself. I wanted to study with those who have learned who they really are and demonstrate this realization for others with their whole body and mind.

After contemplating this question for some time, it came to me that these Zen people were not the way they were by good fortune alone. I came to understand that they all went through a similar training program. Although their training had great variety, it also had a shared quality, which was to use the human body and mind in the practice of sitting upright, silent and still, and to engage in that practice together with others with the guidance of a teacher. This was the opportunity that I saw in Zen training. I saw an accessible, traditional practice of becoming a person such as these ancient and modern Zen people.

Through our wandering, we become more and more ready and willing to meet with others and converse with them about the forms of our training. At some point, we see that wandering away from where we are right now is not going to realize our deepest wish. During this errant journeying, we try to set standards up on our own. Gradually we come to see that this is futile. We begin to understand that we need to enter some form of training to give up running away. We see that we need to include others in our search. Supported by this insight, we are ready to wholeheartedly enter training.

Realizing the light of our original nature goes beyond hearing and seeing and is not within reach of feeling or discrimination. For the sake of this realization, we need training that fully embraces all of our senses, feelings, and discrimination. And in our wandering, it becomes clearer and clearer that we cannot do this training on our own. We need to do it together with others. I heard that the discipline of Zen training fully embraces our senses, feelings, and discrimination. When I heard about the Zen teacher Suzuki Roshi and his community, I thought that they might provide what I was looking for.

4

Diving Deeply into Training

AFTER COMING TO SAN FRANCISCO ZEN CENTER and being supported to practice,[1] I was able to practice diligently on a regular basis. Then I found that I had difficulty with the practice itself. I often found the practice to be really hard, especially the sitting. In the wonderful silence and stillness of formal sitting, I often had both physical and emotional pain. I was afflicted with pain in my knees and back and hips. I also experienced various challenging emotions. I noticed various kinds of grasping and resisting in the midst of sitting. And if by compassionately embracing those afflictions they became temporarily quiet, I often experienced the arising of an even more challenging and subtle affliction: boredom. I have heard from others that they experience boredom too. This is a common occurrence in Zen practice.

When I was at Zen Center in the fall of 1968, I heard that Suzuki Roshi was going to teach the *Lotus Sutra*, so I started reading it in preparation for his teaching. When I read the parable about the poor child shoveling dung, I thought it was a great metaphor for what I was going through in my practice. I thought I was like that child. Reading the parable, I was encouraged to see my practice was included in the teachings of the *Lotus Sutra*. For me, the image of dung shoveling has a deep resonance with the painful challenges that arise within sitting meditation. Over the years, I've come to see and feel that our physical and emotional difficulties, like dung, fertilize and enrich our practice of compassion.

In the parable, after the son settled into his dung shoveling and became more confident, the father came to him in the stables dressed in dirty clothes and said, "From now on you shall be just like my own son." He asked his son to stay and work there. At this time the father also sent old servants to be his son's companions and to help his son in the work. The father also gave his son a new name and new clothing as one would to a beloved child. Giving a name is a further example of the father's skillful means. Although the son did not know it, the father was secretly giving him a precious jewel. Name giving is a vital thread running through the bodhisattva path. It is described in the *Lotus Sutra* and many other scriptures of the Great Vehicle.

Observing the son's hard work, the father assured the son that he didn't have to worry about anything anymore. He saw how his son had been working and praised him for diligently practicing the precepts of right livelihood. He commended his son for not being lazy, deceitful, grouchy, greedy, or angry. In doing so, the father was transmitting the family precepts to his son. At the heart of this statement, I hear the father saying that the son is just like him.

The dung in the stables of the parable can be found in the Zen meditation hall, the teacher's room, the kitchen, and our whole personal and interpersonal world. These are the realms where we learn to embrace our suffering and let go of our resistance to it. We also learn that we cannot accomplish this work alone. We see that we have coworkers who help us in the work, just as the son had companions to work alongside him. In this work we learn to be compassionate to ourselves and others in our afflictions and thus discover what we really are. When we become more experienced in this work, we will be able to accept and enter the more subtle work of our family business, which is awakening to the intimacy that is our true nature.

The forms and ceremonies of Zen training are set up to help us work intimately together with our teachers and our community. Just as in the parable, in our training we are supported, supervised, and accountable to others. This is not about self-control or about being controlled by others. The support, supervision, and accountability are mutual. Intimate mutuality is the compassionate heart of Zen training.

In the process of our training, when we are ready and willing to express our wish to receive the bodhisattva precepts, we make our request to a teacher, a preceptor who will practice with us in the stables of the temple. Generally speaking, it seems that in Asia when people enter training in a Zen temple, they either have already received bodhisattva precepts, or they receive them when they enter the temple. In the West, it seems quite different. People usually start practicing sitting meditation either at home or in a temple before they have formally received the bodhisattva precepts.

In my case, I practiced sitting for quite a while before I even heard about these precepts. I did not think about receiving precepts until I heard there was going to be a ceremony, and then I thought maybe I could join that great event. I didn't know much about the precepts at that point, but it seemed they were part of what Suzuki Roshi was offering, and I was up for whatever that was.

I've heard from many people that when they heard about the bodhisattva precepts, they thought and felt that formally receiving and practicing them would be supportive of their practice and beneficial for the world, and a wish arose in them to receive the precepts. When the wish to receive arises, and one is ready and willing to express that wish, it is traditional to make a request to a teacher, a preceptor who will give the precepts and practice with us in the stables of the temple.

In this process, we are given a name and a Buddhist robe and the precepts. These are three priceless gifts. The Sixteen Great Bodhisattva Precepts may be expressed as follows:

THE THREE REFUGES

Taking refuge in buddha
Taking refuge in dharma
Taking refuge in sangha

THE THREE COLLECTIONS OF PURE PRECEPTS

Embracing and sustaining the precept of discipline
conducive to liberation
Embracing and sustaining all good
Embracing and sustaining all beings

THE TEN MAJOR PRECEPTS

The precept of not killing
The precept of not taking what is not given
The precept of not misusing sexuality
The precept of not lying
The precept of not intoxicating the mind or body
or self or others
The precept of not speaking of the faults of others
The precept of not praising self at the expense of others
The precept of not being possessive of anything,
especially the dharma
The precept of not harboring ill will
The precept of not disparaging the triple treasure[2]

Initially these precepts, along with the name and the robe, are equipment for people entering bodhisattva training. Our understanding of the teachings of the name, the robe, and the precepts will evolve over time. And what are the precepts? At the beginning it might seem that they are rules we follow that are given to us by someone else. In our maturity, we see that they are the truth of our original home. In fact, they *are* our original home.

Throughout our ongoing training with the name, the robe, and the precepts, there will be many opportunities for discovering the jewels hidden within these gifts. We will talk about the evolution of understanding of the name that was given to me in several different places in this and later chapters. In the next chapter we will unfold teachings of the robe.

Although we usually don't see this at first, our new name is a subtle intimation of our original nature and a prediction of buddhahood. Receiving and practicing with our new name, clothing, and the precepts is a formal way to enter into the process of awakening to who and what we really are. Working intimately with the bodhisattva precepts brings our dung shoveling to maturity.

After I had been shoveling dung in the stables of Zen Center for some time, Suzuki Roshi gave me a new name. This is just like the father in the *Lotus Sutra* giving a new name to his son. He gave me the name Tenshin Zenki, priest clothing, and the sixteen great bodhisattva precepts. At that time, he also gave me a simple teaching about the name. He said, "*Tenshin* means Reb is Reb," but I did not comprehend the significance of this gift. Since then, I have continued to explore and discover precious and powerful teachings embedded in the name. New revelations keep coming day after day, year after year. And just like in the *Lotus Sutra*, all of these revelations come of themselves without seeking anything. In our training, we just keep shoveling the dung of our afflictions and discovering pearls. It is like the following story of Zen Master Dongshan and his teacher, Yunyan:

> *Dongshan said to his teacher, Yunyan,*[3] *"I have some habits that are not yet eradicated."*
>
> *Yunyan said, "What have you been doing?"*
>
> *Dongshan replied, "I have not even concerned myself with the four noble truths."*
>
> *Yunyan said, "Are you joyful yet?"*
>
> *Dongshan said, "It would be untrue to say I am not joyful. It is as though I have grasped a bright pearl in a pile of dung."*[4]

The bodhisattva does not find the pearl in a pile of jewels. The joy of the bodhisattva is not simply to be surrounded by joy. It is also to be surrounded by an ocean of affliction.

Before we receive the bodhisattva precepts in the formal ceremony of giving and receiving, we practice confession and repentance of our beginningless greed, hate, and delusion. Confession and repentance are essential in the practice of shoveling dung. This compassionate process of confession and repentance has the power to remove the obstructions to the precious teaching of the dharma. It is a truthful practice wherein we learn to acknowledge and become intimate with our mistakes and feel sorrow with regard to them. Sincerely practicing in this way protects all beings. It is said that this is the pure and simple color of true practice, the true mind of faith, and the true body of faith. In this practice we are inconceivably helped.

All activities become dung when done to gain something. When we try to get something out of our life or practice, affliction is omnipresent. Being out of touch with our original nature, a sense of destitution naturally arises. From this sense of imagined destitution we become concerned about gain and loss. The sense of destitution together with a sense of a separate self with concerns for gain and loss constitute a self-perpetuating cycle of affliction. The more intimate we are with the afflictions of this cycle, the more we are able to be free of the afflictions. This is essential work for students of Zen. As in the parable, this work goes on for a long time. It is actually endless.

Bodhisattva precepts are fundamentally true awakening. They are expressions that flow forth from Buddha's great compassion. But sometimes when we are learning to practice them, we may think that they are about personal purity and become rigid about how we are shoveling with the precepts. At such a time, a teacher, a spouse, a child, or a friend might compassionately teach us a thing or two about how we are missing the point. I suggest that the ethical precepts of Zen are to joyfully and wholeheartedly join hands and walk together with all living beings through the inexhaustible brambles of suffering.

As we acknowledge and recover from our sense of destitution, we become ready to discover and accept the unfathomable intimacy of our original nature. In the process of recovering, we also continue to confess and repent the shortcomings in our practice to show others how to shovel and recover. Then we become like parents who lovingly deign to work alongside their children in the stables of our lives. Wholeheartedly shoveling dung along with others, we realize an intimacy that is true peace.

Our ancestor Liangshan worked in the stables with his teacher Tongan. He served as his teacher's attendant, and part of his job was to carry the teacher's robe:

> *One day as Liangshan was handing his teacher the patched robe, Tongan said, "What is the business beneath the patched robe?"*
>
> *Liangshan did not have an answer.*
>
> *Tongan then said, "Studying buddha and still not reaching this realm is the most painful thing. Now, you ask me."*
>
> *Liangshan asked, "What is the business beneath the patch robe?"*
>
> *Teacher Tongan said, "Intimacy."*[5]

At the beginning of our three-month monastic Zen training periods, we have an initiation ceremony that is called *tangaryo* in Japanese. *Tanga* means "itinerant monk," and *ryo* means "room." In some of the monasteries in China, Korea, and Japan, when monks came and wished to stay temporarily, they would go and sit in the room for itinerant monks. Also, if they wished to enter the community in a long-term way, they would start in the tangaryo in order to intimately harmonize with the monastic environment and the human community. In doing so they also demonstrated their determination to enter the practice. In the classical examples of ancient times, the length of time was usually indeterminate; it came to an end when the teacher and the community were satisfied that the student sincerely wished to enter the monastery.

Nowadays, we continue to offer a formal period of several days for this initiation. At the very entrance to the monastery, we go through an intense form of training in giving up our attachment to comfort and to having things go our own way. This period of initiation is a wonderful opportunity for the students to intimately experience their self-centered concerns. They may be greedy and impatient for this initiation period to be over and may feel aversion to the difficulties of it, but by being still, patient, and courageous with all this, they become free of their resistance. It does sometimes happen that self-concern drops away in the moment, and students find themselves just sitting without trying to get anything out of it. In such cases, shoveling dung gives rise to pure and sweet fruit. In the bodhisattva way, training in intimacy goes on indefinitely, formally and informally.

Even after this intense initiation, the deeply ingrained habit of grasping and trying to get something for ourselves continued to resurface for many of us. When we were sitting, many of us found that we were trying to get something out of it. Perhaps we were trying to get ourselves under control. Perhaps we were attempting to acquire the ability to do extraordinary things or to enter into extraordinary states of being. Or perhaps we were just trying to get through the day without too much suffering. Now I see that all of these thoughts of getting something are just examples of dung that we are called to shovel. Mature practice is sitting upright and being intimate with our deluded thoughts of trying to gain something from our practice.

On a cold and rainy Sunday morning in the mountains during my first practice period at Tassajara, my work assignment was to dig a hole in the earth. While digging in the earth the thought arose that at that moment some of my friends back in San Francisco may have been sitting comfortably in a warm and good-smelling coffeehouse drinking coffee, eating pastries, and reading the Sunday paper. And here I was in a situation I had voluntarily entered and paid for so that I could dig in the mud in the cold rain. I wondered about this form of Zen training. I found it questionable, but I didn't give up because somehow I knew even then that the heart of Zen training is questioning the training itself. Now I feel the truth of this even more deeply. All the forms of practice to which I am wholeheartedly devoted should be called into question.

In practicing mindfulness of breathing, I got involved in another kind of affliction. I slipped into trying to control my mind by counting my breath. I did act like this, but I did not do it on my own *and* I accept full responsibility for it. I was being mindful of my breathing, and the thought arose that I could get something out of this.

Gradually I became aware that among my student cohorts there appeared to be an imaginary hierarchy among the different forms of mindfulness. For example, there were the people who counted their breath. They were at the bottom of the hierarchy. Then there were those who followed their breath. They were in the middle. And then there were the people who just sat. They were at the top. This was an opportunity to make things more interesting, to have a little competition rather than just sitting and training in Zen together. One could attain some local fame by being the first person on your block to just sit.

But all along I also heard the ancient admonition: "Don't fall into gaining ideas. Don't get into climbing the hierarchy of practices." And yet we were trying to do that very thing. Trying to get something out of the practice is not in accord with the bodhisattva ethical precept of not taking what is not given.

Maybe because he was aware of the competitive and comparative ways that we were practicing, in January of 1970, Suzuki Roshi suggested that we all go back to basics and do the same practice of counting our breaths, one to ten, and again, and again. I think he wanted us to understand that becoming intimate with our breath is just sitting.

About seven months after he told us all to do the same practice, one of my dharma siblings said to me, "Remember when Roshi told us all to do the same practice of counting our breaths?"

I said, "Yes."

He said, "You don't think he wants us to continue, do you?"

I said, "I don't know."

And he said, "Do you think it's okay if we go on to a more advanced practice?"

I said, "I don't know." And I still don't.

In a hierarchal practice, one might start by becoming well-grounded in sitting upright and counting the breath. Rather than doing the supposedly more advanced practice of just sitting, one might try to get really good at counting breaths. Becoming skillful in breath counting need not involve any gaining idea. But we might slip back into making mindfulness of the breath into a gaining enterprise. In the process of training in intimacy, we might repeatedly slip back into our wandering contrivances to get something. Such regression is part of training. This is some of the dung that we must shovel. The purpose of our shoveling is not to become the leader of the dung shovelers. But that human impulse to become the best might arise among breath counters, and breath followers, and among just sitters.

Before Suzuki Roshi gave us all that basic instruction to count the breaths, I set myself on a crash course to become a perfect breath counter. I tried to control my mind into being completely fixed on breath counting. As I approached perfection, I realized this is not what I wanted, and I gave up that way of practice. This is a realization that came to a dung shoveler. More than fifty years ago, I gave up trying to get something from sitting. Since that time, I've tried to be compassionately aware of any attempts to gain something in the practice of seated meditation. I often remember Suzuki

Roshi encouraging us to wholeheartedly sit without trying to get anything. However, this does not mean we don't receive great blessings in our practice. It's just that we are not *trying* to get anything out of it.

This way of practice may be less dramatic and less worthy of being made into a soap opera or a Broadway play. It might not seem interesting to just sit when we're sitting, and just walk when we're walking, and just eat when we're eating. But such simple practice is intimate with what we really are, wherein we realize the peace and harmony of our true nature. Our practice is to be kind to what is happening now without seeking anything, including not seeking to be famous for not trying to get anything. Still, we might slip into the dung of the affliction of wanting to be above average in our great practice. Or we might become afraid of being below average.

In my first formal meeting (*dokusan* in Japanese) with Suzuki Roshi in 1968, when I was sitting cross-legged on the floor in front of him, he said something like, "Your breathing is quite natural." I felt he was saying, "That's the way to breathe. You're breathing the way you should breathe." He didn't say that I was doing some technique properly, and he didn't instruct me in any technique. He didn't encourage me to get better at breathing. He didn't tell me to get better at counting my breaths. He just said, "You are breathing quite naturally." I was breathing in the way I was breathing. I felt that he was telling me right then, in our first formal meeting, that I was breathing naturally and breathing naturally was good. At that time, I felt he was approving of my practice.

Now I understand that he was telling me, "You're breathing naturally just like me. I breathe naturally too. I'm just like you." He was saying, "You are my child. You're what I'm here for. The way you breathe is what I'm here for. The way I breathe is what you're here for. The way we're breathing together is what we're here for."

I didn't trust and understand this at the time, so more work with dung was needed. Not understanding the intimacy and deep intention of his kind teaching, I was vulnerable to slipping into a gaining approach.[6] I got obsessive about counting my breath. I tried to get myself under control so that I could count my breath without missing a beat. I thought being good at counting my breath would mean never losing count. And finally, by being a rigidly controlling dictator with my practice, I didn't lose count. In other words, I slipped from just shoveling to trying to get my shoveling under control. When I finally arrived at almost complete control, I could see that was not what I came to Zen practice for. I came to Zen practice to learn to be like those wonderful Zen ancestors who were open, relaxed, flexible, and generous. I was just becoming more uptight, closed, and stingy in this way of practicing. I came for something wonderful, and I got distracted. Such dramas, however, were more opportunities for shoveling dung. When I saw the futility and unkindness of trying to control myself, I gave up practicing in that way. From then on, I trusted being aware of my posture and breathing as they naturally occurred. Without trying to, I came into accord with Suzuki Roshi's kind teaching.

All those thoughts and innumerable other forms of dung are wonderful opportunities for compassion. This is the whole universe working together in the form of dung shoveling. Whatever dung arises, we just wholeheartedly shovel and give up trying to be in control of the dung or the shoveling. I don't know if I will ever come to the end of this.

There is an endless variety of dung. One of the main forms is the delusion that we are separate from complete, perfect awakening, that we are separate from the buddha way. Can we just keep shoveling without trying to get anything and simply continue our practice? In this practice, we don't deny or try to get rid of our attitudes; we examine them compassionately. This is the art of dung shoveling. In learning this art, when afflictions come up, we might think, "I should become better at this. I should be better than other people at this. I should get some appreciation or approval for this." When we get caught by such thinking, it is simply another opportunity to learn the art of shoveling dung.

After practicing a while, I had the happy thought, "What am I doing with my life just sitting here, dealing with my body and mind? I'm not accomplishing anything." It occurred to me that it was strange that a young person would devote (some would say waste) the prime of their life to just sitting in silence and practicing together with others in community. But training continued in the face of such questions. The training was to simply be present and concentrated, and I was devoted to that. Still, it occurred to me that this was an unusual and questionable way for a young person to be living.

I remember Katagiri Roshi mentioned that at the time Sawaki Kodo Roshi died, there was an article in a Japanese newspaper about him. The headline said, "Zen Master Wastes His Life Sitting in Meditation!" After he told this story, Katagiri Roshi commented, "That's pretty good!" That story encouraged me to live my life that way too. It was encouraging that someone could say that I was wasting my life like he did. Sitting still in a cold meditation hall hour after hour and shoveling mud in the cold rain, I sometimes wondered if I was wasting my time. My friends and family back in Minnesota might have thought so. But I just wondered, and I still don't know.

In the summer of 1970, Suzuki Roshi asked me and another young man to help him move rocks in a garden he was creating at Tassajara. He asked us to move one particularly large rock from where it was sitting over a few feet. And then he asked us to move it to another spot a few feet away. And then he asked us to move it again to another spot a few more feet away. We did that all day long. At the end of the day the rock was pretty much in the same spot where it had been at the beginning. I thought it was a wonderful day with our teacher and a great teaching, and I am still grateful for it.

The practice of shoveling dung does not require achieving anything. When we deal with our thoughts of gain and loss long enough, we may become ready for a teaching that there is nothing to gain or lose. We have nothing to attain because we are already what we truly are, which is complete and perfect. But we must shovel to fully appreciate such a complete, perfect, and subtle teaching. When we enter and engage in the endless practice of reality, we must be able and willing to go back to the beginning and just shovel dung.

For example, I was offered the great honor and opportunity to serve the community as head monk at Tassajara for a ninety-day practice period after I had practiced at Zen Center for about five years. And what was my honored work assignment? It was to clean the toilets, to collect and shovel compost, and to recycle the garbage. This is traditional work for the esteemed position of head monk. Here we can see the intimacy of Zen practice.

After some time of expedient practice, compassionately shoveling the afflictions of greed, hate, and confusion, we become soft, flexible, upright, and open to the real practices that are given to us. Then we are able to practice from the perspective of our original nature. In this way, we are weaned from thinking that we do not include everything in the whole universe and that the whole universe does not include us. Herein we contemplate and realize that we are just like buddha, and buddha is exactly like us. We are thus, and buddha is thus too. To enter this reality, we need to be thoroughly kind to our habit of trying to get something out of life and trying to be something other than what we are right now.

5

Unfolding the Gift of the Robe

WHEN THE DESTITUTE SON IN THE PARABLE reencountered his father after his long period of wandering, he didn't recognize him and he was awestruck at the majestic power and wealth surrounding this person. He was frightened and trembled at the prospect of what might happen. He thought, "This is not a good place for me. I could be captured and forced into labor." So he ran away again. The parable suggests that we become destitute and desperate in our search for who and what we really are when we wander away from where we are. Even though we are wandering in destitution, we will get another chance to encounter our original nature by means of various causes and conditions. However, without training, we will be intolerably awestruck and terrified. Thus, we will be unable to appreciate and enter the beauty of this wondrous relationship.

Later in the parable, the father thought of expedient means to entice his son to come back. After a long apprenticeship in shoveling dung, the son will gradually recover from his destitution, alienation, and sense of inferiority. His confidence will grow, and he will finally be able to accept his original nature with all its responsibilities.

In the process of our wandering, we do sometimes fortuitously glimpse an aspect of something awesome. We might receive some intimation of what we are really looking for in life. However, without preparation we might not be able to open to this radiance.

I say that we wander away, but we only wander away in our dreams. Similarly, we dream of returning even though we never really left. When we return in our dreams, we don't necessarily like it or feel like it is home. If we're not sufficiently trained, we will not be able to face the awesome mysteriousness of what we really are. Training our body and mind to fully embrace all experiences is the process through which we will become able to tolerate the ungraspable, unthinkable, unnamable reality of our original nature. We might experience that beauty as the face of something so awesome and so mysterious that we tremble. Training our body and mind in relationship to these issues is the process of realizing our true nature.

One of the glimpses I had of what I was looking for came during my first visit to Zen Mountain Monastery at Tassajara in the summer of 1967. I heard about Tassajara from a close friend who was living and practicing there, and I went to visit him about one month after the monastery opened. Although the mountains were stunningly beautiful, I didn't like the valley. I found the sulfur smell of the hot springs to be stinky, and there were so many flies buzzing around my face! Sometimes when we first see what we are looking for we are both attracted and repelled.

Ironically, not too long after that I thought, "Maybe I'll go live there." Later that fall, I went to San Francisco to sit at Zen

Center and to meet Suzuki Roshi. In that meeting, I was given another glimpse of what I was looking for.

When I met Suzuki Roshi, the first things I saw were his feet. I was sitting on the floor in the meditation hall at Sokoji Temple in San Francisco where he taught.[1] I was looking at the floor, and his bare feet walked by. When I saw his feet, I thought, "These feet can teach me Zen." As we left the meditation hall after that period of sitting was over, each of us met him on the way out, face-to-face. We joined our palms and bowed to him, and he joined his palms and bowed to us. When I bowed to him, I looked at him, and he looked at me. Then his eyes turned away.

In this short period of time, many questions arose in my mind about what had happened. I wondered, "Was I not supposed to look at him? Was he offended? Was he frightened of me? Did he dislike me? Did he like me?" There were so many possibilities. So much was going on. I was struck by the ambiguity of the meeting, but I felt quite comfortable with it. As I walked away, I thought, "Oh yeah, this seems right." In this first meeting with the teacher, I felt like, "Yeah, I think this is a person with whom I can explore training mind and body." I was encouraged to meet him again and again.

I've told this story about his feet many times. Sometimes when I tell it, people ask me, "What was it about his feet?" Well, they seemed clean and well cared for. As they landed, each foot seemed really present with the floor. At the time I saw his feet, I wasn't exactly thinking all this, but I was looking for a teacher who could teach me with his whole body and mind, and it seemed that his whole body and mind were teaching me. His feet could teach me. His hands could teach me. His face could teach me. I had the great good fortune to be taught by Suzuki Roshi's body and mind for about four years before he died.

When our dear teacher was around, we could bask in the warmth of his presence, and in his presence, we were all on our best behavior. In the joy of practicing with him, we may have taken him for granted and not have felt the urgency to practice the teachings he offered to us. However, after he left us, we did understand that we had the responsibility to carry on his teaching, and we began to accept the opportunities of adulthood in the buddha way.

Today I feel that Suzuki Roshi acted as a guide beyond the guidance we receive from our families on the path of realizing our original nature. My dear, sweet father, for whom I am very grateful, could not offer me the training I was looking for; Suzuki Roshi did. This training opportunity was not something I set up on my own. In my adolescence, I tried to do so. My advisor tried to help me set up my training, but I didn't want to enter the training he offered. Suzuki Roshi showed me training opportunities that were in accord with what I was looking for, which was to respond appropriately in all circumstances. Thus, my period of adolescent wandering was gradually passing away, and I was getting ready to enter into the work of adulthood.

In July of 1970, when I was with my teacher at Tassajara, the thought occurred to me that, since he was a priest, it would be appropriate if I was a priest too. So I went to him and requested ordination. It was as simple as that. One month later, I was ordained as a Zen priest by Suzuki Roshi. Just as the father in the parable gave the son new clothing when he entered into the work of the stables, I was given a new robe when I was ordained as a priest. When I received this robe, I did not imagine the rich teachings it would bring to life.

After I was ordained, I asked Suzuki Roshi's wife, whom we called Okusan,[2] to order a linen robe (*okesa*) for me. Originally, the robe was black. About fifteen years later, after completing formal dharma transmission, I was given some brown robes and permission to wear them. Later, I had the idea to bleach my nice black linen robe. When I did, it came out a lovely, uneven, almost mangy, dull brown color. This was a result of my endeavors, which were part of my training. However, I didn't do a very good job of bleaching it. As a result of my color-changing activities, the fabric was weakened, and it started to fall apart in various ways—and it continues to fall apart. For more than fifty years, I and many other people have been trying to repair and maintain this fragile robe. A couple of years ago, a kind person skillfully sewed a new backing on it. The new backing is holding the robe together, so it's quite a bit heavier now. The front continues to need ongoing repair but quite frequently, when people see this delicate robe, they say it is beautiful. Even though what they're seeing is a motley robe that is falling apart, this falling-apart robe gives people an opportunity to see beauty. Part of its beauty is in the variety of the stitches where we can see the kindness of many people.

It is easy for me and others to see that this old robe is falling apart. We may not realize it, but what we are seeing is a robe that is in an open-ended process of deterioration, change, and renewal. This robe is not permanent and is not annihilated. It is a superficial, perceptible appearance of our profound, imperceptible, original nature.

When I'm wearing this robe, people have an opportunity to open to things falling apart: the robe and me. If they can endure this awesome falling apart, they will experience its beauty. However, if we can't tolerate things falling apart, we close the door on reality because things *are* falling apart. They're not falling apart into annihilation; they're falling apart into bits and pieces of the entire universe.

The way we are falling apart and becoming the whole universe, and the way the universe is falling apart and becoming us, is our original nature. This is the reality of our life and death. If we can be present and endure the terror of this tremendous process of falling apart and becoming that is the reality of our life, this process will appear to us as beauty.

Everything is turning into infinite parts all day long, and all day long infinite parts are turning into things. This process is our true nature. And so, we work to develop the ability to live as what we truly are and to tolerate the terrible beauty of wreckage and renewal. T. S. Eliot asks, "Where is there an end to the drifting wreckage?"[3] In our original nature, there is no end to us and no beginning of us. We're not something that is completely intact that comes to an end and becomes a wreck. We are vaster and more ambiguous than that. It is in the midst of this vast ambiguity that truth comes into our awareness as beauty.

Opening to and enduring the awesome, overwhelming aspect of things is simultaneously opening to their beauty and truth. Ironically, we sometimes say that something is beautiful in an attempt to protect ourselves from its real beauty. Doing this, we close the door on the unmanageable and inconvenient reality of our life. We might say that something or someone is beautiful to avoid the fear of really meeting them. Once, Suzuki Roshi surprised me by saying that to call something beautiful is a sin. Calling things beautiful might be a way to minimize them in an attempt to make them manageable by putting them in a "beauty box." We also use the word *cute* for similar purposes. It could be that someone or something we comfortably call "cute" suddenly becomes much more than cute. At that moment the door of mystery might open, and we might feel terror.

I remember Suzuki Roshi saying that our sitting practice (zazen) is a great tenderizer. In our Zen bodhisattva training, we become tender, flexible, and imaginative like children so that we, too, can have the opportunity for initiation into the vastness of reality. Since childhood, we have been learning techniques to hold the vastness of reality at bay, but right now we have the opportunity to let go of those techniques at least temporarily. In this regard, we need to learn to be more soft, flexible, upright, and honest like children. Children and adults do sometimes feel a need to feel safe. We need to allow and be allowed to say, "Stop that!" In this way, the world can come back together, and we temporarily turn away from what scares us.

What we really are is a relationship. It is a process in which everything is included in us, and we are included in everything. The son in the parable was awestruck by his first glimpse of his father's home and tried to run away. Like him, we may resist and want to run away from the teaching that our original family is the inconceivable process of our reciprocal inclusion with all beings. We might think, "I'm not included in him. He's not included in me." We might resist this complete reciprocity, but when we do, our resistance is also part of the process of realizing it. Without training and guidance in developing generosity, ethical discipline, and patience, we cannot develop the confidence to accept the truth of this teaching of reciprocal inclusion.

One of the fundamental characteristics of phenomena is that they change. They are impermanent. When we hear such a teaching and we open to it, we may feel some fear. When we can be with the way things are impermanent, when we open to the possibility of some beloved form of life being on the verge of changing or at risk of being wrecked, it is natural to be awestruck. When we can tolerate that awe, we simultaneously open to beauty. This simultaneity is very subtle, and even its subtlety is awesome. We can barely stand it in a balanced way, balancing between turning away and touching it. The subtlety is also beautiful, but there is no beauty if there's no awe, if there's no terror, if there's no trembling, if there's no mystery. We need training to be still and patient with this mysterious trembling. This is not to get the beauty; the training is to be with reality, which has a beautiful aspect and which is inseparable from fear. Facing the fear in stillness and silence realizes truth, which sometimes comes to us as beauty.

My precious younger grandson died accidentally when he was seventeen years old. At the time of his death, when someone asked me, "How are you?" I said, "I'm full of life and death."

As the ancient teacher Yuanwu[4] wrote,

Birth is the manifestation of the whole works.
Death is the manifestation of the whole works.
Filling up the great empty sky,
Upright heart[5] is always bits and pieces.[6]

Our family was grieving the loss of the life of this beautiful boy and simultaneously dealing with the beginning of a terror we could barely tolerate. When this boy was alive, we were not so aware of the terrible aspect of his beauty. His tragic death opened the door to an unbearable terror and beauty. In our relationship with those we love, there's no way to really hold on to self or other, and any attempt to do so walls off love. In the process of attempting to control things, if we face the terror of losing our hold in these relationships, the wall of separation starts to crack. When we open to that crack and compassionately meet how we feel with that crack, beauty and truth emerge. This beauty is not our idea of beauty because our idea of beauty just cracked.

The full experience of beauty and truth includes feeling and accepting our human vulnerability. But vulnerability may also be frightening. We may feel that the universe is going to overwhelm us and gobble us up. The universe consumes us. That's part of reality. It also includes us gobbling up the universe. The universe is vulnerable to us too. This reciprocal vulnerability is our true nature, and it is awesome. In the beginning of that awe, beauty is glistening.

The moon poet Saigyo wrote,

This leaky, tumbledown
Grass hut left opening for the moon,
And I gaze at it
All the while it was mirrored
In a teardrop fallen on my sleeve.[7]

There are training methods to enable us to tolerate being a leaky tumbledown grass hut and to allow the light of the moon to penetrate our wreckage. We have the opportunity to train by taking care of things so that they show us our mutual vulnerability. Training helps us to be present with our potentially frightening vulnerability. It enables us to be present with our impulses to deny it or run away from it. Training is not to "get" beauty. Training is to become able to tolerate the terror of vulnerability and to open to the beauty of the moon.

This moon just happens to be beautiful if we accept and realize that we and the moon are always on the verge of breaking, of changing without being annihilated. Looking at the moon may be exquisitely painful as we accept our mutual impermanence. When the beauty comes, terror comes with it.

There is sometimes a sentimental view of children that sees them as perfectly enlightened buddhas. Buddhas always respond spontaneously, free of thought, and children sometimes do so too. If you call to a buddha, the buddha's head turns. If you call to a child and their head turns, the child is just like the buddha. But sometimes when you call to a child, they may respond like an ordinary sentient being: frightened, confused, and entangled in their thoughts.

A truly wonderful love often arises between grandparents and grandchildren, but sometimes the grandparent's adoration of the grandchild may seem overwhelming to the child. If the grandparent is sensitive and alert to this possibility, they can help the grandchild find and express the boundaries of their tolerance for the intensity of such adoration. In this way, the grandchild can settle with and explore this radiance, this love, this moonlight. Feeling the moonlight shining, the grandchild might feel, "It's getting too intense. I need a break." And if the grandchild can express that need, the grandparent can accept it and give them a break from the moonlight.

One time as I was watching my grandson with great adoration while he was eating his breakfast cereal, his brow furrowed deeply. He said to me, "Would you stop staring at me!" So I looked at the ceiling instead of him. I turned the light of love up toward the ceiling, and he could relax and return to eating his cereal in peace.

Like the grandchild opening to a grandparent's love, we may also learn to open to the moonlight of great compassion that is shining both on us and through us all the time. Through training in this way, we learn to remember and accept the fragility and radiance of our impermanent home. The light of our original home is always illuminating our impermanent home. Not realizing this, teardrops may be shed, each of which reflects this great light.

Sometimes we might need to take a break from the moonlight in order to open to it more fully and consistently. Learning to take breaks that we need might require having a mentor who helps us and allows us to ask for breaks. This requires a conversation between mentor and student like that between grandparent and grandchild.

In the revelations that come to us in the process of wandering, we see our inability to fully accept the radiance of our true nature. Seeing this, we understand the necessity for guidance. We may have to wander quite a long time, and sometimes we may have to get into big trouble before we're able to say, "Okay, I need help, and I want it." After we have wandered around long enough, after we've become destitute and impoverished enough, eventually we will enter training. When we do formally enter this path, sometimes it will be really intense and difficult. Doubts may arise about continuing it. In the long path of training, we might sometimes need breaks. The dung we need to shovel may be heavy and have a strong odor, and our back may hurt from shoveling it. This training may be hard, but we might be up for it because we know from experience what it's like to wander alone, unsupervised, unemployed, and deeply attached to our ideas. Both wandering and training are difficult, but the first is endless suffering and the second is the path of awakening.

6

Entering the House

BY TRAINING IN JUST SITTING, free from any gaining ideas, we develop confidence in our true nature and are ready to enter into the dynamic dance of our original family. At this point we can pivot from the limited work in the stables to the unlimited activity of the great house. Entering the great house is the time when we turn from individual effort to practicing together with all beings and the great earth. In formal practice the first steps in our pivoting are to practice intimately, inquire, and listen to a teacher.

In the face-to-face transmission of our family business, we realize the nonduality of the work in the stables and the work in the treasure house. We become ready to accept the responsibilities of our family business, and we enter mature, adult practice. Now, we transition from working for the family business to accepting responsibility for the family business.

In "Guidelines for Studying the Way," the Old Buddha Dogen wrote,

> There are two ways to penetrate body and mind: studying with a master to hear the teaching and devotedly sitting zazen. Listening to the teaching opens up your conscious mind, while sitting zazen is concerned with practice-enlightenment. Therefore, if you neglect either of these when entering the buddha way, you cannot hit the mark.[1]

Dogen spoke of two ways to enter deeply into the body and mind of real practice. The first way is just sitting (*shikantaza* in Japanese), just being our self, without adding or subtracting anything. The second way is going to meet the teacher, requesting and listening to the teaching (*sanshimonpo* in Japanese). In the first, we trust the self; in the second, we trust the other. The first is intrapsychic; the second is interpersonal. As we go back and forth between just sitting and meeting the teacher, these two modes are balanced, harmonized, and unified. In this way, we deeply penetrate and settle into our true family business.

I have discovered that this teaching by Dogen is contained in the name *Tenshin Zenki* that was given to me by Suzuki Roshi. *Tenshin* may be translated as "naturally real." It may be understood as the self settling into the self in wholeheartedly sitting. *Zenki* may be translated as "whole works." It is the whole universe, and it is the whole universe working in the particular form of going to meet the teacher and discussing the dharma face-to-face.

Classically, when students entered the Zen family business, they would go to a teacher and formally request guidance in buddhadharma. Meeting the teacher face-to-face, they would offer incense and prostrations. This was understood as a ritual gesture of formally and respectfully asking for the teaching. Beyond this nonverbal request, a student might say, "I respectfully ask for the teacher's compassion. Please give me teaching."

Once a laywoman asked me, "Is there a formal way for me to ask someone to be my teacher?" I told her that in some Zen temples, at the beginning of seven-day meditation intensives (*sesshin*), participants go into the teacher's room, offer incense and perhaps some other offerings, perform three prostrations, and then they face the teacher and ask, "Will you be my teacher for this retreat?"

I also told her about another ceremony, which I have been practicing with priests for many years, that is to go to the temple and greet the teacher at the beginning of the year, usually on January 4. Upon entering the temple, the student places a formal statement on the altar requesting the teacher to teach in the coming year. Then they greet the teacher face-to-face, and the teacher and student do three prostrations to each other. Then they wish each other "Happy New Year" and do one more prostration to each other. There may or may not be some informal exchange of good wishes also. I told her I would be happy to do this same ceremony with laypeople. Since that time, I have been doing that ceremony with both priests and lay bodhisattvas every year. The formal statement, which is usually handwritten, may say something like this:

> I respectfully offer you happiness in the new year. I humbly ask for your guidance again this year. Teacher, Old Buddha, I practice with your protection. I pray for your health in body and mind, unlimited prosperity, long life, peace and

tranquility in your temple, and all good fortune. I pray for this with my whole heart.

Although a ritual like this is not always explicitly stated at the beginning of Zen stories, I imagine that, because it almost always did happen, it was simply not mentioned sometimes. Ironically, when a monk did not follow this formal procedure, it would be so remarkable that it would be recorded as a major element in the story.

Here's a case of a monk entering the treasure house to meet a teacher, Zhaozhou, where the sincere request for the teaching is implicit.

The monk asked, "Are we the same or different?"

Zhaozhou said, "We're different."

The monk asked, "What's the difference?"

Zhaozhou said, "You are used by the twenty-four hours, I use the twenty-four hours."

In this rendition of the story, I do not hear the monk asking, "How do you use the twenty-four hours?" But if someone came and asked that question of me, I would say that the way to use the twenty-four hours is to be upright in each moment. Then I might ask the person, "How do you use the twenty-four hours?" Conversing in this way, we use the twenty-four hours, and we are used by the twenty-four hours. In this way Zhaozhou and the monk were the same, and we are like this too.

If we are not upright, the twenty-four hours use us. When we are not upright, we yield to our inclinations. Indulging in our inclinations and prejudices, the twenty-four hours use us. Not being upright with our biases and prejudices, we get stuck in them. We are tossed about by them all day and all night long. Whereas if we are upright, we can use everything appropriately. No matter what happens, we come upright. No matter what we call it, no matter how we turn it, we leap free and respond appropriately. Even if we are getting used, we can be upright with being used. Uprightness is like a pearl rolling on itself in a bowl. The pearl is never upside down or right side up. It is always turning on itself; it is always upright. When we are upright like a pearl rolling in a bowl, we use the twenty-four hours. When we use the twenty-four hours, we meet Zhaozhou face-to-face, and we realize our original home.

Hearing this story, one might think that using the twenty-four hours like Zhaozhou is better than being used by the twenty-four hours like the monk. One might even think that the great Zen master was better than the unnamed monk. However, real practice is not so. In the real practice, Zhaozhou and the monk using and being used are in conversation, rolling on each other like a pearl in a bowl. Uprightness is not stuck in uprightness. It freely pivots with being out of balance.

We can use this story about Zhaozhou to test uprightness. If we cling to any idea, even the idea of being upright, this story challenges us. It calls us into question. Uprightness is an unbiased attitude toward all things; it is the way to realize this story all day long.

In our family business, being upright is practiced in conversation together with our teacher and all beings. We sit upright in the context of genuine conversation with others.

Our practice of being upright is also being accountable to others. We need to be called into question by others. In my early days of practice, a friend told me that he had a dream. It was a dream of us having a party during our sitting in the meditation hall. He said it was just like our usual way of sitting upright, facing the wall, except that since it was a party, we could turn and talk to our neighbors. That was the Zen party he dreamt of: sitting upright and still being in conversation.

Being upright in conversation is the entrance into our original home. Again, what is our original home? It is how each thing is pivoting with everything and vice versa. It is the way we imperceptibly accord with all things, and they accord with us. Nothing is self-produced; everything is in a process of mutual dependent co-arising. The gate into this totally dynamic reality is upright pivoting. We are not and cannot be upright by ourselves alone. Uprightness is not something we do by ourselves. It occurs in concert with the whole world. Being upright is the awareness of the mirrorlike quality of our experience. In fact, the ancestors sometimes called this kind of awareness the jewel mirror samadhi. This is awakening by way of giving and receiving together with all beings.

In the thoroughly dynamic environment of our family business, meeting a teacher in genuine conversation is practiced together with upright sitting. This interpersonal practice of being taught by and teaching others is practiced together with intrapsychic personal work. Thus, we are able to use the twenty-four hours and also be used by the twenty-four hours. I wonder if the old buddhas Zhaozhou and Dogen would agree with this.

When I contemplate the image of being upright in this way, I am reminded of another image of uprightness from ancient India. This image was given by the sublime teacher Nagarjuna,[2] the founder of the Middle Way school of Indian Buddhist philosophy (*Madhyamaka* in Sanskrit). In his teaching of this middle way, he encouraged bodhisattvas to give up the assertions that our life experience arises from itself, from an other, from both self and other, or from neither self nor other. Being upright is to leap beyond all such assertions about our experience. Being upright is just like this. These are basic instructions on how to conduct conversations in the treasure house of buddhadharma.

Turning the Dharma Flower

Once upon a time, the Sixth Ancestor of Zen, Huineng,[3] met a monk named Fada who bragged that he had chanted the Lotus Sutra *three thousand times.*

The ancestor replied, "Even if you chant it many thousands of times, if you don't understand it, you won't understand your misunderstandings either."

Then Fada said, "In my stupidity, I have only been able to follow the words and chant the Scripture. How can I understand the truth of it?"

Huineng responded in verse:

"When your mind is deluded, you are turned by dharma flowers

When your mind is awakened, you turn the dharma flowers."[4]

Buddhas who abide in unsurpassed complete awakening are not restricted to only turning the dharma flower in awakening. They completely include being turned by the dharma flower in delusion. Unsurpassed complete awakening is not only turning the dharma flower in awakening. It is also being turned by the dharma flower. All buddhas are both turning and being turned. This is the pivotal activity of all buddhas. This is the active pivot of all ancestors. This whole book is for the sake of you and me turning the *Lotus Sutra* and being turned by it. It is the enactment of being turned by the parable in delusion and turning the parable in awakening.

7

Compassionately Studying Karmic Consciousness

THROUGH SKILLFULLY INVESTIGATING karmic consciousness, ultimate reality is revealed. In the parable of the destitute child, I see what is called dung as referring to our ordinary karmic consciousness and the shoveling of dung corresponding to our studying karmic consciousness. By "karmic consciousness" I mean our ordinary consciousness where a sense of self appears. This type of awareness may also be called egocentric or self-conscious awareness. It is the kind of awareness where there is a sense of a self, a sense that I am here, I am this, I own this, I do this. This is the mind where karma lives.

The Sanskrit word *karma* has almost become an English word, and there are many different understandings and misunderstandings of it. The Sanskrit word *karma* is usually translated into English as "action." Buddha defined *karma* as *cetana* (Sanskrit). *Cetana* can be translated into English as "intention," "thinking," "volition," or "will." Here, intention refers to the overall pattern, topography, or tendency of a moment of consciousness. The word *karma* is not applied to nonvolitional actions like a knee reflex or salivation. The Buddha taught that *karma* is of three types: mental, physical, and vocal. Mental action is the source; it comes first and may or may not be extended into physical and vocal action. Further, the Buddha taught that actions (*karma*) have three qualities: wholesome, unwholesome, or neutral. Wholesome actions have beneficial consequences, unwholesome actions have harmful consequences, and neutral actions have unclear consequences.

Right now, in this moment of our consciousness, there is a sense of "I," and this consciousness has an overall pattern that includes sense data, feelings, perceptions, a variety of emotions, and discriminating awareness all arising moment by moment. It is an awareness where there is a sense of the presence of a self and an awareness of an appearance of others. This is a teaching of the buddhas that can be observed, experimented with, and tested in each moment of consciousness. One can test the depth of water with a pole and the depth of dung with a shovel. The depths of the mind are tested with words and gestures.

Again, what is karma? It's the shape of each moment of consciousness where there seems to be an "I." Every moment of karmic consciousness has an overall pattern. This pattern may be wholesome, unwholesome, or neutral. And the buddhas say that this activity, this karma, moment by moment, always has consequences.

The medium of exchange in karmic consciousness for humans is language. Even a highly cultivated person might be tossed about in the currents of language. In Zen practice one learns to use words freely without being bogged down or caught by them. We also learn how to talk to others in ways that help them become liberated from the traps of language.

We need to enter and embrace egocentric consciousness before we can fully enter the family business of awakening. The following verse from the classical Zen poem "Song of the Jewel Mirror Samadhi" offers us further instructions for studying the suffering of deluded consciousness.

Move and you are trapped;
miss and you fall into doubt and vacillation.
Turning away and touching are both wrong,
for it is like a massive fire.[1]

The study of karmic consciousness—the observation of it and the experimentation with it—is not just an intellectual exercise. This observation and experimentation are for the sake of embodying great compassion. To develop compassion, we need to study our karma, which is the pattern of our thinking. Studying our consciousness with compassion matures and purifies our compassion. In the buddha way, we learn to observe our thinking compassionately.

Guishan was Yangshan's teacher.[2] We often judge teachers by their fruits, and we will see the sublime fruitfulness of Guishan as we study the teachings of his successor, Yangshan. Yangshan was such an important disciple that one of the five schools of Zen, the Guiyang school, combines his name with his teacher's. Yangshan was nicknamed Little Shakyamuni. He had a number of awakened male and female disciples, and there are many stories about him in the *Book of Serenity* and elsewhere. One of these stories, called "Guishan's Active [Karmic] Consciousness," goes as follows:

> *Guishan asked Yangshan, "If someone said to you, 'All sentient beings just have active consciousness, boundless and unclear, with no fundamental to rely on,' how would you prove it in experience?"*
>
> *Yangshan responded, "If a monk comes,*[3] *I call to him, 'Hey, you!' If the monk turns his head, I say, 'What is it?' If he hesitates, I say, 'Not only is their active consciousness boundless and unclear; they have no fundamental to rely on.'"*
>
> *Guishan said, "Good!"*[4]

In wholeheartedly studying teaching stories, our body and mind dialogues with the story, both inwardly, or intrapsychically, in silent meditation and interpersonally in conversation with others. We go back and forth between inner and outer conversations with the words of the story. We can approach the story as though we are in dialogue with it without contriving or forcing the dialogue. We simply offer our question as a gift and listen for a response.

For example, when we studied this and other stories from the *Book of Serenity*, we sometimes performed them theatrically. In this case, some people played Guishan, some people played Yangshan, and some people played the monk. Sometimes they switched roles to see how that worked. We asked questions, we listened, and we responded. Sometimes we responded literally using the words of the story and sometimes differently. In this way we enacted the stories interpersonally.

It can also be fruitful to have an inner, intrapsychic dialogue with the words of the story. For example, the first line of the first verse commentary in the *Book of Serenity* is "The unique breeze of reality. Can you see it?" When we contemplate that line of verse within our individual psyches in silence and stillness, questions may arise: What does it mean to see a unique breeze? Do I hear it? Do I feel it? And if I don't, who does? Questioning the story and being questioned by it takes our investigation deeper and deeper into the truth of the story.

Both questioning and listening can be offered as gifts. We can do this without trying to get anything. A response to our effort will come naturally, free of our expectations. The response is not separate from our inquiry; they come up together. We turn the story, and it turns us in the process of study. We are in intimate relationship with the story. The commentary on the story and the story itself also turn on each other, and we will become more aware of this dynamic dance as we continue to study.

In the story of Guishan and Yangshan, I see two skilled teachers working closely together to explore and test a student's understanding of karmic consciousness and to probe with words and gestures how the student works with the dung of karmic consciousness. I also see their great compassion for the student. They converse in this way to help students discover and realize the mind of wisdom right in the midst of the confusion of karmic consciousness. The story also demonstrates the compassion of the father in the parable who is repeatedly testing his son's faith and readiness in the midst of karmic consciousness. This story describes Zen training through a conversation between these two teachers and in our study of this conversation we join this process of training.

Karmic consciousness is the mind in which there is a deceptive appearance, an image, an idea, a feeling, or some other sense of an independent self. Simultaneously with the illusory appearance of a self, a delusion arises that the self is the actor, the thinker, the controller, or the director of the activities of consciousness. This story focuses on and studies karmic consciousness. It offers us an opportunity to explore the ambiguities of karmic consciousness in detail.

Hearing this teaching about karmic consciousness, some people might feel afraid or discouraged. However, accepting the description of karmic consciousness as having no fundamental to rely on allows us to enter into the way that this deluded consciousness pivots with the immutable knowledge of all buddhas. If karmic consciousness was substantial and had a foundation, then it could not pivot with inconceivable ungraspable perfect wisdom. If it had a foundation, we would be in big and permanent trouble.

Probing and testing consciousness are essential elements in the process of realizing its true nature. The true understanding of karmic consciousness is the mind of wisdom. This wisdom mind is both intimate with deluded karmic consciousness and free of it. Both personal and interpersonal exploration are essential to realizing a mind of wisdom that pervades karmic consciousness as the intimate interfusion of delusion and awakening. Through compassionate investigation of karmic consciousness, we can awaken to the pivotal activity of delusion and awakening. This pivotal activity is our birthright, our original nature and our family business is the practice of realizing who we truly are. In this way, we carry on the family business.

Guishan states that karmic consciousness is boundless, unclear, and has no fundamental to rely on. Then he asks Yangshan how he would test someone to verify that their experience in karmic consciousness is like that. In verifying that karmic consciousness is unclear, wisdom is realized.

In response to Guishan's question, Yangshan said, "If a monk comes, I call to him, 'Hey, you!'" This is the first test. If the monk's head turns without hesitation, it turns just like buddha's head would turn. The monk is not bothered by being called in that way or by wondering what he should do. He just responds like buddha. At this moment, the monk is liberated from karmic consciousness and demonstrates it by turning his head.

If someone passes this first test with flying colors, Yangshan would probe deeper. We can see what a thorough examiner of karmic consciousness Yangshan is in what he says next. He offers another test by saying, "What is it?" If the monk falls for this and hesitates, he temporarily falls from the richness of liberation that he just demonstrated back onto the destitute and rutted road of habitual thinking. Failing Yangshan's second test, the monk demonstrates that karmic consciousness is boundless and unclear, and there is no fundamental to rely on. In this way, Yangshan shows how we may be both caught by and liberated from karmic consciousness. He further shows us that even if we pass the first test and are liberated at that moment, since there is no fundamental to rely on, we might not pass the second one.

In commenting on this story in the *Book of Serenity*, Wansong brings up another story:

> *A monk asked Yunan, "The* Treatise on the Flower Ornament *says that the fundamental affliction of ignorance itself is the immutable knowledge of all Buddhas; this principle is most profound and mysterious in the extreme, difficult to comprehend." Yunan said, "This is most distinctly clear, easy to understand." At that moment a boy happened to be sweeping there. Yunan called to him, and the boy turned his head. Yunan pointed to him and said, "Is this not the immutable knowledge?" When Yangshan calls a monk, and the monk turns his head, that is precisely this situation. Yunan then asked the boy, "What is your buddha-nature?" The boy looked around, at a loss, and left. Yunan said, "Is this not fundamental affliction?"*
>
> [In commenting on this second story Wansong says,] *"If you can comprehend this, then you become a buddha immediately." The boy's bewilderment and the monk's hesitation are no different. The fundamental affliction of ignorance and the boundless, unclear, active consciousness are also the same. When Yunan and Yangshan examined monks and tested people, they accomplished their aim in this way.*

All these teachers—Guishan, Yangshan, and Yunan—were investigating ordinary karmic consciousness to discover the nonduality of delusion and awakening. First, they tested students by calling to them. If the student demonstrates liberation in the midst of karmic consciousness, then they tested again for deeper verification. Yangshan said, "What is it?" Yunan said, "What is your buddha-nature?" Can you see the vital thread of compassion running through their probing? These ancient teachers expressed their compassion by calling students into question.

In both of these stories we can see that ignorance and buddha's wisdom are never separate and are always pivoting with each other. This is the immutable knowledge of all buddhas. It is itself complete liberation.

This liberation is karmic consciousness free of hesitation or second-guessing. No more, no less. Being buddha is us being completely the way we are in that moment. Our assignment as buddha is to be the person we are completely. We are constantly changing. We are different in every moment, and buddha is no different from each of us being completely who we are, moment by moment. Being buddha is being wholeheartedly the way we are, and it is not limited by the way we are. Whatever and whoever we are, buddha is us wholeheartedly being what we are, which includes the great earth and all living beings.

In his verse commentary on the dialogue between Guishan and Yangshan, Hongzhi turned the story and offered us the following verse, interweaving this Zen story with the *Lotus Sutra* parable. In this verse, I see the intimate, reciprocal activity of our original nature. In our original nature, delusion and wisdom intimately dance together and liberate each other. Whether we see it or not, the bright moon of wisdom shines through the tangled vines of deluded consciousness.

One call, the head turns—know the self or not?
Through ivy, the moon becomes a hook.
A child of thousand-fold gold, as soon as he falls
Vaguely, on the road of poverty, has distress.[5]

"One call, the head turns" reflects Yangshan's skillful calling "Hey, you!" to the monk to test whether or not the monk is free in the midst of self-centered consciousness. If the head simply turns, the freedom of the buddhas is demonstrated. In this turning of the head, we have the moon of wisdom shining through the ivy of karmic consciousness.

Then Hongzhi says, "Know the self or not?" This is the same as Yangshan saying to a monk, "What is it?" After the turning of the head, Yangshan kindly offers a second test. If the student hesitates, he is hooked and falls onto the road of poverty. Hongzhi comments, "A child of thousand-fold gold, as soon as he falls, vaguely, on the road of poverty, has distress." Here again we see the destitute child in the *Lotus Sutra* losing touch with his original nature and the father's compassion for his sorrowful plight.

Hongzhi also offers the comment, "Through ivy, the moon becomes a hook." He doesn't miss a chance to show us the interfusion of passing the test and failing the test. He wants us to see the interpenetration and nonduality of the full moon of wisdom and the hook of delusion. When the moon is full, where is the hook? When the hook is present, where is the full moon? The verse demonstrates the phases in the life of wisdom pivoting intimately with the life of delusion. When there is delusion, where is awakening? When there is awakening, where is delusion? These are the kinds of questions that we deal with when we enter the house and assume adult responsibility for the family business.

In our family business we have the responsibility to explore the teachings about consciousness and the opportunity to discover the reality of our life. The eminent teacher Miaoxin[6] demonstrated how to be responsible in this way. She showed how to use words to compassionately test and encourage understanding. Her teaching demonstrated the wonder-working possibilities of the student-teacher relationship. Interacting intimately with students, she taught how to deeply penetrate and liberate karmic consciousness. Because of her heroic aspirations, great diligence, and strength, she was recommended to serve as a senior official in Yangshan's monastery. Yangshan appointed her to serve as director of the guest quarters near the entrance of the monastery. She took care of relations with visiting monks, nuns, lay practitioners, and government officials.

Taking care of these various guests offered Miaoxin the opportunity to help people awaken to the true nature of mind and objects. On one occasion she had the opportunity to teach people about the famous story about the Sixth Ancestor, Huineng. When Huineng was a guest in a monastery, he heard a group of monks arguing about whether the wind moved or the banner moved. He famously said to the monks, "It's not the wind that moves or the banner that moves. It is the mind that moves."

> *There was a group of seventeen monks from Shu, in the west, who were on the road in search of a master. On their way to*

climb up to Yangshan's monastery, they stopped and stayed at the guesthouse. While they rested in the evening, they discussed the story about the wind and the banner of Huineng. . . .

Miaoxin, who overheard the discussion from outside the room, said, "How wasteful! How many pairs of straw sandals have these seventeen blind donkeys worn out? They haven't even dreamed of buddhadharma."

Her assistant worker told them that Miaoxin had not approved their understanding. Instead of being upset with her disapproval, the monks were ashamed of their lack of understanding. They got formally dressed, offered incense, bowed, and asked her to teach.

Miaoxin said, "Come closer."

When the seventeen monks were getting closer Miaoxin said, "It is not that the wind flaps. It is not that the banner flaps. It is not that your mind flaps."

Hearing her words, all seventeen monks had realization. They thanked her and formally became her students. Soon after, they went back to Shu without ever climbing up to Yangshan's monastery.[7]

Miaoxin used words to test the seventeen monks' understanding, and they all passed the test. It seems that they never did meet the great teacher Yangshan directly but, in fact, they did meet him through his great, compassionate disciple Miaoxin. Meeting Miaoxin was enough.

Our precious human life is embraced and sustained by three types of mind: karmic consciousness, an unconscious mind, and a wisdom mind. Our life is embraced by and, in turn, embraces these three forms of awareness. In studying the first two deeply, wisdom is realized. The function of wisdom is to embrace, illuminate, and liberate the other two forms of awareness. Embracing and illuminating occur in the silence and stillness of concentration. Our life is the oneness and reciprocity of our body and these three minds.

8

Exploring Mind and Environment

NOW LET US LOOK AT ANOTHER STORY about Yangshan exploring and testing a student's understanding of karmic consciousness. This story, called "Yangshan's Mind and Environment," offers us several more teachings about how to study consciousness, observe its dynamic contents, and notice if there is kindness in the observation process.

Yangshan's conversations with the student are like the father's instructions to the poor son on the subtle workings of the family business. Both Yangshan and the father use provisional teachings and skillful means to help the next generation discover the real truth of the family business. In both cases, the real and provisional teachings are pivoting on each other. What is provisional is that we have to learn the family business. What is real is that we are already and we always have been full members of the family of awakening. There is no difference between the provisional and the real, but it might seem that there is.

Introduction to the Story

The ocean is the world of dragons—disappearing and appearing, they sport serenely. The sky is the home of cranes—they fly and call freely. Why does the exhausted fish stop in the shoals and a sluggish bird rest in the reeds? Is there any way to figure gain and loss?

The Main Story

Yangshan asked a monk, "Where are you from?"

The monk said, "From Yu Province."

Yangshan said, "Do you think of that place?"

The monk said, "I always think of it."

Yangshan said, "The thinker is the mind and the thought-of is the environment. Therein are mountains, rivers, and the land mass, buildings, towers, halls and chambers, people, animals, and so forth; reverse your thought to think of the thinking mind—are there so many things there?"

The monk said, "When I get here, I don't see any existence at all."

Yangshan said, "This is right for the stage of faith, but not yet right for the stage of person."

The monk said, "Don't you have any other particular way of guidance?"

Yangshan said, "To say that I have anything particular or not would not be accurate. Based on your insight, you only get one mystery—you can take the seat and wear the robe. After this, see on your own."[1]

Earlier we discussed how to penetrate a teaching with body and mind, both inwardly through upright sitting and interpersonally in conversation with a teacher. Having received a teaching story and having deeply contemplated it by sitting upright in silence and stillness, we can go even deeper into it through conversation with another person.

In the intrapsychic realm of just sitting there is a dynamic interaction with the teaching. After we receive the teaching, we work with it intimately and drop everything. When we do this, the story freely turns and resonates with our whole body and mind. Settling into this resonant awareness, we enter the dynamic intrapsychic reality of the teaching. Entering the reciprocity of interpersonal awareness, we discover the reality of dependent co-arising.

In his introduction to the story, Wansong says, "The ocean is the world of dragons—disappearing and appearing, they sport serenely. The sky is the home of cranes—they fly and call freely." Who are these serenely playful dragons and freely flying cranes? What are they? Cranes and dragons are metaphors for the creatures of the buddha way.

I propose that they represent our wondrous activity when we have realized our original nature. By engaging in the intimate workings of the family business, we learn who and what we really are, and after doing so we continue with our family business so that all sentient beings may also realize their original nature.

Then Wansong asks, "Why does the exhausted fish stop in the shoals and a sluggish bird rest in the reeds? Is there any way to figure gain and loss?" Who are these exhausted fish in the shoals and sluggish birds in the reeds? They are you and me before we have trained in the family business and discovered who we really are. They are you and me when we're caught trying to be other than who we are right now. They are you and me when we're sunk in our concerns for gain and loss.

The fish is exhausted in a dream of being something other than a fish, perhaps trying to be a dragon. We could say the fish wanders away, but it only wanders away in its dreams. How wonderful it would be if the fish accepts its exhaustion completely. The acceptance of this exhaustion is not theoretical. It is the alert admission of it. Then the fish can wake up to being a dragon. It is the same for the bird; it's all pooped out and dull, its energy depleted because it has spent so much of it messing around and holding on to its thought activity. The bird has become sluggish because of its worldly endeavor to figure out how to become a magnificent crane. Is there any way to figure gain and loss?

One Sunday after I came to San Francisco to practice Zen, I went with friends to Ocean Beach. I had seen the Pacific Ocean before in Los Angeles and Mexico but had never gone swimming in it. That Sunday I did go swimming, and it was a lovely swim. After a while, I decided to swim back to shore but even though I was swimming quite strongly, I noticed that I wasn't getting any closer. I swam harder but still made no progress. I started to become concerned about gain and loss. I raised my arms in the air and called to my friends, but no one seemed to see or hear me.

I noticed that the harder I tried to swim back to shore, the more frantic and exhausted I became. I looked away from the shore out at the vast ocean to the west, and I thought, "If she wants me, she can take me." I felt as though the ocean was my great mother, supporting my life, and yet she might be taking it away now. I thought that this might be the end of me. There was a growing feeling of resignation, mingled with another subtle sense that there might be more to my life than this day. I don't know that I consciously said to the ocean, "I surrender." I don't remember thinking or saying that, but in retrospect I think that I did surrender.

I stopped swimming and gave up trying to get back to shore. I think I might have lost consciousness, and I'm not sure how long that went on. Suddenly, I was startled into consciousness as if from a dream. I felt my feet touch the sand. I thought that if that happened again, I would try to push on the sand with my feet. I didn't even think of swimming. When my feet did touch the ground again, I pushed against the sand. And then again and again.

Finally, I found myself in water shallow enough for me to crawl out onto the sand. Then I collapsed, like an exhausted fish, face down on the beach. Lying on the sand, I heard a little boy say to his mother, "Is he dead?" She said, "I don't know. Maybe." Then I heard the sound of a siren, and I thought, "Oh, that might be an ambulance coming to get me," and then I thought, "I don't want to be touched by strangers and taken to a hospital." So somehow, I got up and started walking back to where my friends were. They did not know what I had been through, but I was alive and I was awestruck by being alive.

Why does the exhausted fish stop in the shoal? Is there any way to figure gain or loss? For days I walked around San Francisco seeing people going here and there, and I wondered if they realized the preciousness of their lives. I was like an exhausted fish, and being like an exhausted fish was not that bad.

If we practice unconstructed and imperturbable stillness and silence with whatever kind of fish or bird we are, we leap beyond concerns for gain and loss and enter the realm of dragons and cranes.

Having played with the introduction, now let's enter into the depths of the main story. All of Yangshan's words in this story are meditations and contemplative instructions that take the form of questions and statements.

> *Yangshan asked a monk, "Where are you from?"*
> *The monk said, "From Yu Province."*
> *Yangshan said, "Do you think of that place?"*
> *The monk said, "I always think of it."*

Earlier, we considered a conversation between Yangshan and his teacher, Guishan, in which they discussed how to probe and test a student's understanding of karmic consciousness. Now we can go even deeper into Yangshan's teaching by turning our attention to the conversation in this story. The case itself presents basic teachings on the nature and function of karmic consciousness. It also gives instructions about how to study consciousness and the self that lives within it. The story also shows us how this student faithfully receives, practices, and partially attains the liberating potential of these instructions.

Here is a student who I imagine is ready to approach the teacher Yangshan from the silent depths of his upright sitting.

He is ready to begin a conversation with the teacher in the treasure house of Zen. I see that the student in this story had already trained in the provisional practices that the parable speaks of as dung shoveling.

Shoveling is studying and practicing with the dung of karmic consciousness. We develop maturity and confidence by becoming intimate with the dung through our shoveling. Through this training, the student in the story became somewhat free of karmic consciousness and had the confidence to approach the teacher with an open heart and mind without trying to get anything from him. Thus, the student was able to enter the treasure house and listen to the precious teachings and put them into practice.

Yangshan also invites us to discover where we come from, that is to say, our original nature. It doesn't say so in the original text, but I'm imagining a disciple who met the teacher and respectfully asked for the teaching. I see the teacher's words as a response to this sincere request.

Yangshan asks the student, "Where are you from?" This question could be taken at the literal level of Yangshan asking what earthly place the monk comes from, but I would like to look at this question as Yangshan asking the monk to turn the light around to illuminate his karmic consciousness. He is probing the monk's understanding of the process of karmic causation from whence the student, a conscious human being, has come. The student responds by saying "from Yu Province." He might have been literally referring to a geographic place and at the same time, it can also be understood as referring to his karmic consciousness.

When Yangshan asked, “Do you think of that place?” he was actually asking, “Do you think of the unconscious storehouse of all your past karma from whence you come?” I understand the monk’s answer, “From Yu Province,” as code for the consequences of his past karma. The disciple wisely said, “I always think of it.” What else is there to think of?

Alternatively, Yangshan could have asked, “Do you think *from* that place?” And again, the student could have answered, “I always think from that place.” Here, we see Yangshan’s way of probing and testing the student’s understanding of the history and consequences of his karmic consciousness.

In the conversation between Yangshan and this student, I see a shared understanding. I think they understood that whatever we think now is based on what we have thought before. The consequences of our past thinking, our past karma, is stored in our body and unconscious cognitive processes. In other words, our present karma is based on the consequences of our past karma. Our current consciousness arises in dependence upon these unconscious processes. Moment by moment, this is where we come from. This what the student was referring to as “Yu Province.”

Our thinking, gestures, and vocalizations are always new and fresh. They have never happened before. But what we are consciously doing is given to us by unconscious processes wherein our past action is recorded and embodied. We always recycle old material into our fresh thinking. We always think based on the consequences of our past thinking. We move forward into the future looking through a rearview mirror.

When the student tells Yangshan where he comes from, he is also telling him about the objects in his consciousness. So Yangshan tests the student to see if he understands this by asking, "Do you think of that place?" And the student understands Yangshan's intent and says, "I always think of it." Our thinking is *always* based on where we have been before. Our thinking always comes from and is based on our embodied unconscious, the storehouse of our karmic history. For example, our ability to think, speak, and write in English is based on and is a consequence of innumerable past actions of listening to and learning to speak English. A child who does not have much past karma of this sort cannot think, understand, or speak fluently. As we get older and our bodies change, our ability to remember and to think and express ourselves in English also changes.

Where do we come from? We come from our own past karma and also the past actions of others. The past is past, and yet it is always embodied in our present unconscious awareness. The embodied consequences of our past actions are the foundation of our present conscious mind and all the objects that appear within it.

After examining the monk about his understanding of where he comes from, Yangshan then taught about the dynamic inner workings of ordinary karmic consciousness. Yangshan said, "The thinker is the mind and the thought of is the environment. Therein are mountains, rivers, and the land mass, buildings, towers, halls and chambers, people, animals, and so forth."

Within karmic consciousness there is karma, there is activity. This activity usually includes the appearance of a thinker and that which is thought of. The thinker is nothing in addition to thinking, although it may appear to be that way. And also, thinking is nothing in addition to what is thought of. None of these three exist independent of each other, and none can be grasped separate from the others. Seeing the ungraspability of the whole situation and each particular within it is seeing the dharma body of buddha. On the other hand, grasping a thinker as separate from or in addition to thinking and that which is thought of is the fundamental affliction of karmic consciousness. These interdependent aspects of the whole activity of consciousness dependently co-arise.

Thinking is the activity of karmic consciousness in which thinker and that which is thought of, self and object, mind and environment, appear and disappear together. The self co-arises and coexists in consciousness with thinking and the objects of thought and it is nothing in addition to them. Although it might appear that someone or something is doing the thinking, that appearance is a delusion. Grasping this delusion is affliction. Even our language, which is the medium of exchange in karmic consciousness, offers expressions like "I think" and "my thinking," and so on. In this way, language maintains and supports believing the delusion that "I" do the thinking. Nothing does the thinking.

Although Yangshan doesn't say so explicitly, I think he knew that both thinker and that which is thought of (the environment) dependently co-arise together and cannot be grasped separately. He teaches us that conscious knowing is composed of active subjects and passive mental objects. Yangshan called the active side "mind," and he also taught that the passive side of mind might appear as material things—for example, mountains, rivers, and earth. Although he didn't say it, he could have also said that the passive side of mind might appear as nonmaterial objects like feelings, perceptions, ideas, emotions, dreams, fantasies, and intuitions. Although Yangshan speaks of "mind and environment," they are equal aspects of mind. Yangshan is trying to teach us the reality of mind and object.

The Chinese character used here for "thinking" is composed of two other Chinese characters. One is the character for "field" or "rice paddy." The other is the character for "mind" or "heart." The character for "thinking" could be interpreted as "the field of mind" or "the pattern of mind." As we said earlier, this character is also used to translate the Sanskrit word *cetana*, which means the overall pattern of a moment of consciousness. This overall pattern is the definition of the karma of a moment of consciousness.

The environment that appears in karmic consciousness, which is always deluded, is composed of the objects of thought. Although Yangshan didn't articulate it, the objects of thought within consciousness are mental, even though they may appear to us to be both mental and material. Yangshan's instruction sets up the realization that everything that appears within consciousness is just mind. The entire universe *as we think of it* is just the passive aspect of karmic consciousness. The entire universe gives rise to our karmic consciousness, but our karmic consciousness cannot comprehend this arising. Although deluded consciousness is supported by everything outside itself, it cannot think of anything outside itself no matter how hard it tries.

The activity of thinking and the objects that are thought are equal and intimate partners within consciousness. Subject and object are always present in deluded consciousness. The conscious mind is manifested and understood in the dance of thinking and its objects. Realizing this dance also realizes that there is no thinker separate from that which is thought of and no subject separate from object, no dancer in addition to the dance. In the realm of this realization, karmic consciousness is illuminated and liberated. Yangshan is training the monk and us for the sake of this liberating realization. In other words, Yangshan is teaching us who and what we really are.

The father in the parable of the destitute child is like Yangshan. He's trying to teach his son who and what he really is. Others show us who we are. When we study who we are together with others, we begin the wondrous work of understanding and doing true justice to others. If we try to understand others without studying ourselves, we will be unsuccessful. And similarly, if we try to understand ourselves without listening to others, we will be unsuccessful.

For example, once when I was in Japan in the 1970s, I went to an art school to meet one of the teachers there who was a sculptor. My intention was to invite him to come to San Francisco Zen Center to sculpt a life-size statue of our founder Suzuki Roshi. He accepted the invitation and came to Zen Center. He created a wonderful statue. After it was completed, Katagiri Roshi, one of our teachers, said the sculptor was thinking of portraying Suzuki Roshi, but because he didn't take into account his own thinking, the sculpture ended up being a projection of himself and his thinking. In other words, if we try to portray others without including the study of ourselves, we just wind up portraying ourselves and not doing justice to the other. If we want to do justice to others, we need to study our self and engage in wholehearted conversation wherein our portrayal of others can be called into question. Genuine conversations bring thinker and that which is thought of into question.

We are a conversation. If we wholeheartedly contemplate what we think the self is, we will become aware of how completely other-dependent it is. The real life of the self intimately includes all the others that it is dependent upon. This is the original nature of the self. The way to be intimate with others is to be completely what we think we are and to offer this to others in genuine conversation. When we welcome what appears in consciousness in the form of a self or an other, we can engage in conversation that is fully alive and liberating. Such conversation is what we really are.

Deeply studying and compassionately conversing is the path of freedom in the midst of the delusions of self and other. In thoroughly conversing with an other, we awaken to the equality of self and other. This meeting is not necessarily comfortable, and it might not be in accord with our previous views of ourselves and others. We are like the child in the *Lotus Sutra* who, in conversation with his father, became disabused of his previous views of himself and his father.

Every "other" affirms and completes us, but we might not see that yet or even want to see it. Some others tell us who we are in a way that goes along with who we think we are. That could feel good, but it might not help us understand the reality of self and other. It might only reinforce our dreams of who we are. If we wish to awaken, it's good to know that we are dreaming. When our dreams are reinforced or confirmed by others, we might remain unaware that we are dreaming.

Sometimes after I give a talk, people come up to me and say, "That was really a good talk. That's what I think too!" And when they say that, I think, "Uh-oh, are my words just confirming people's habitual ways of thinking?" On the other hand, when I give a talk and no one says anything one way or the other, I might also feel that my thinking and speaking and gesturing are all called into question. And then if someone tells me that they disagree with what I offered or that it was unhelpful, that feedback also calls me into question. All three of these situations are opportunities to be called into genuine conversation. Feeling called into question in these ways is the kind of conversation that can free us from our egocentric, karmic enclosure and realize justice for all beings.

Karmic consciousness is an impoverished enclosure. Within this enclosure, conversations like that of Yangshan and his student show us how to give up our belief in the separation of thinker and thought. The way we become free of this belief is through compassionate conversation with others. This is also the path of becoming free of the illusion that self and others are separate entities.

We are paradoxically identical to what is not us. How we really are is both self *and* other. Everything we are not fully includes us without confining us. Fully accepting this, we realize who we are.

These are all opportunities to understand the intimacy of Yangshan's thinker, thinking, and that which is thought of and the harmony of mind and environment. However, if there is a hairsbreadth's separation between thinker, thinking, and that which is thought of, between mind and environment, the door of liberation is closed.

9

The Pivotal Activity of All Buddhas

THE TEACHING AND PRACTICE of ALL BUDDHAS and ancestors is the pivotal activity of the whole universe. It is the intimate activity of buddhas and sentient beings turning with each other. It is the turning of mind and environment, the pivot of thinking and that which is thought of. It is the turning of the dharma wheel and being turned by the dharma wheel. In the previous chapter, Yangshan introduces this pivotal activity by his teaching "reverse your thought to think of the thinking mind—are there so many things there?"

Now let's look again at Yangshan's instruction. He encourages us to look and think freshly about how we think. His instruction can be seen as an invitation to and an instruction in introspection. It is offered to help us discover the inconceivable truth of our conscious experience. Just as the father in the parable invited his son, Yangshan is inviting us to enter the house and learn the family business. The father wanted his son to learn the comings and goings of the house. Teaching and learning the intimate relationship of mind and environment is the family business of Yangshan's house. Now, we will see the student, like the son, beginning to learn the business of Buddha's house.

The buddhas and ancestors offer expedient means—in this case, skillful psychological teachings—for the sake of discovering the truth of how the mind works. How we think and what we think of—the objects of our mind—is what Yangshan called "the environment."

Whether we think of past, present, or future or mountains, rivers, people, feelings, or frogs, all these appearances in consciousness are mentally constructed. What we see is a mentally constructed world. The appearances of all these things that seem to be real are illusions that are given to us by our evolutionary history, our language, and our culture.

To investigate and understand what our thinking really is, Yangshan encourages us to reverse the usual pattern of consciousness to observe our present thinking activity itself. Instead of thinking of objects of thoughts, we and the student are instructed to think of the subject of thought, to think of the one who is thinking. We are instructed to reverse the usual pattern of thought and practice mindfulness of consciousness itself. Yangshan is training us on how to discover the structure and functions of thinking (karmic) consciousness.

At the heart of this reversal of thought, we open to a reality that is free and unhindered by mentally constructed objects. In this eternally new reality, there is freedom from the illusion of the duality of subject and object, mind and environment. We are not caught by the delusion that there is a thinker separate from the process of thinking and from the objects of thought.

In buddhadharma, the world of consciously constructed objects, which are mistakenly understood to be reality, is sometimes called the Saha world. The word *Saha*[1] implies an opportunity for patience, or endurance. This is a world in which we have the opportunity to practice patience with the great afflictions that arise from mistaking mental constructions for reality. It is also a world in which we have the opportunity to create more afflictions by getting angry with internal and external afflictions. Training in patience with the suffering of not understanding reality is one of the most important forms of dung shoveling. In this Saha world, we can be very blissful for a certain period of time, but when the bliss ends, it might be painful. And if we're not well-trained in patience, we could easily become irritable and angry. In the painful world of mental constructions, buddhas are required to practice patience. By practicing patience with the pain of misunderstanding reality, we walk the path of compassion and wisdom.

Once, on a sunny spring day in Tassajara, after many days of darkness and cold rain, I was hanging laundry on the clothesline. I hung a piece of cloth, maybe it was a towel, that was bright white as it reflected the sunlight. When I hung the freshly washed laundry and smelled it, I thought, "This is worth it. This moment is worth coming into this life with all its difficulties. If all I get in this lifetime is to hang these clothes on this line and see this light of the sun reflecting off these clothes into my eyes, I'm willing to put up with the rest of it." In that moment, I was given my seat in the world of suffering.

I understand I will die. However, my vow is to come back until the whole works, every little particle of the universe, is willing to be where it is and accept its seat in the world of suffering. That is my vow.

In the story about Yangshan and the student, Yangshan is reaching out to a student who has found his seat in the world of suffering. Yangshan is embodying his bodhisattva vow and encouraging the student to look at life in a new way. When he says, "Reverse your thought," he is saying, "Let's make a radical alteration in the way you're thinking. I want you to take a totally new approach to what's going on in the conscious mind. Relinquish all your usual patterns of thought. Give up your habitual ways of thinking and then think of thinking itself." Yangshan is saying, basically, "Turn from thinking of Yu Province to looking at the mind that is thinking."

Thinking of the thinking mind, there is only the thinking mind. Thus, the thinking mind is relinquished. The mind road is cut off. On this wondrous cut-off mind road, we understand that the ability to think and the objects thought of are not separate. We understand that Yu Province and the one who is thinking of Yu Province are one suchness. We see that mind and environment are one reality, and in this realization mind and environment are mutually transformed. This is how Zen practice transforms the world.

In commenting on the student's statement, "I always think of it [Yu province]," the teacher Wansong said approvingly, "True words—he should confess and repent."[2] "Confession" in this case means the monk is acknowledging the karmic habit of always thinking in terms of his past. The mind that thinks of objects is the mind that projects a self onto objects. This creates the deceptive appearance of objects existing on their own, separate from subjects, and thus setting up grasping within consciousness. The confession and repentance that Wansong encourages is to acknowledge that we are thinking in this way. He further encourages us to repent and reform by following Yangshan's instruction to turn the light of the mind around and illuminate the process of thinking itself, thereby discovering how illusory it is. Following this instruction realizes the intimacy of subject and object, mind and environment. This intimacy is the suchness, the reality of mind and object.

In our usual karmic consciousness, there appears to be an external world independent of our mind. Yangshan told the student to turn this world-projecting ability around and to look back at the mind in which there appears to be an external world separate from itself. Now, we look back at the mind that thinks that what it sees is not itself. Thinking a world is out there existing on its own is the way we usually try to find our way, to find our place. Yangshan offers this pivotal activity as an opportunity to become free from the deeply embodied tendency to project independent existence onto everything.

Almost four hundred years after Yangshan's conversation with this student, the ancestor Dogen offered another version of this teaching when he said, "Learn the backward step that turns the light inwardly to illuminate your self. Body and mind of themselves will drop away, and your original face will be manifest."[3]

Yangshan's teaching in this story is just like Dogen's instruction to learn the backward step. Training in this practice is auspicious for illuminating our original nature. However, in following the instructions of Yangshan and Dogen for learning this backward step, a common emotional response might be frustration. Learning the backward step is revolutionary. It is a radical reorientation of our usual mode of attention that sees objects of thought (thought objects) as external to mind and instead turning the light of awareness onto consciousness itself. So it may feel quite disorienting for some time.

If we feel frustrated or disoriented in this reorientation, the compassionate skills we have learned from long hours of dung shoveling come in handy. The pain of frustration calls for compassion in the form of generosity, careful attention to ethical discipline, patience, diligence, and concentration. Out of concern for later generations, Yangshan and Dogen, like the father in the parable and the Buddha in the *Lotus Sutra*, offer turning words to enter and explore the vast treasure house of buddhadharma.

How do we look back and study thinking itself? Where do we look? When we follow this teaching, we look at our ability to think and, at the same time, we use our ability to think in a new way. In learning this revolutionary form of contemplation, many feelings might arise. In this situation, we might notice that we feel frustrated, awkward, and unskillful in practicing this new way of thinking. Sometimes we might feel as if our mind is short-circuiting or that our head might explode. This is because of the contradiction of trying to think in a new way by using our old ways of thinking.

Our usual way of thinking is dualistic. We think, "I practice; I meditate." What would be new, and perhaps difficult, would be to shine the light back without thinking, "I shine the light." In this reversal, there is a fresh way of thinking, free from the idea of a self that is doing something. However, this reversal from habitual to new ways of thinking may be deeply disturbing. If so, these disturbances might indicate that this teaching has been received and faithfully practiced. We are exercising our ability to think in a radically different way; but we are not used to it, so we might feel uncomfortable. It takes time to integrate and settle into this new and liberating way of thinking.

The common linguistic construction of "I do *x*" reinforces and perpetuates dualistic thinking. Contemplating the duality of linguistic construction, we become more and more aware of how we are turned about and confused in the flow of language. Learning to be upright and balanced in the stream of language helps us to become free from our habitual thinking.

This liberating reversal of our habitual way of thinking is brought to maturity by a further renunciation. This renunciation is to give up thinking of ways to get something out of life, to give our life to the discovery of reality without trying to get anything reverses our ordinary way of thinking. The one who is willing to sit in meditation without trying to get anything is the one who allows wholehearted practice free of seeking. In this reversal and renunciation, our original nature, our original face is revealed. In realizing our original nature, there is no attainment and there is no nonattainment. We have to do a lot of dung shoveling to be able to tolerate the intensity of no attainment and no nonattainment in perfect wisdom.

Yangshan instructs the monk, and us, to reverse the thinking mind and to turn attention inward rather than outward to look at karmic consciousness itself instead of the objects therein. Yangshan suggests that in the midst of thoroughly studying the thinking mind, we realize the intimate pivot of mind and environment. When we engage in this study without concern for gain and loss, the study reveals the nonduality of mind and object. And in this nonduality, the doors of liberation are open. Hearing about the doors of liberation being open, we imagine going through them. However, this cannot be done. In that openness we are called to be very careful, silent, still, and open at the threshold. One whose thought has been reversed in this way is immersed in the endless, ungraspable practice of turning and becoming free of everything in the dharma realm beyond words.

The great teacher Yaoshan[4] also teaches us about the pivotal activity of all buddhas.

> *Once when the great teacher Yaoshan was sitting, a monk asked him what kind of thinking was going on when he was sitting so immovably still.*
>
> *Yaoshan answered, "Thinking not-thinking."*
>
> *Then the monk asked, "How do you think not-thinking?"*
>
> *And Yaoshan said, "Beyond thinking."*[5]

In Yaoshan's immovable sitting, thinking is not-thinking and not-thinking is thinking. Yaoshan's thinking not-thinking doesn't mean that he wasn't thinking. It also doesn't mean that he was thinking of a thing called not-thinking. In the stillness and silence of wholehearted sitting, Yaoshan's thinking was so thorough and dynamic that thinking was pivoting with not-thinking, and not-thinking was pivoting with thinking. Yaoshan called this pivotal activity of thinking and not-thinking beyond thinking.

To be wholeheartedly engaged in some activity is to be engaged in nothing but the activity itself. When our actions are wholehearted, they are upright and nothing is added. In upright action, there is no excess and no deficiency; there is just the action. This thoroughness is not a contrivance. It is immediate practice, and it is immediate realization. It is thinking in which there is nothing in addition to thinking. When thinking is thorough, there is the realization that thinking and not-thinking pivot on each other and thus they are not separate. Thoroughness is the medium wherein thinking and not-thinking turn on each other and leap beyond themselves like a pearl rolling on itself in a bowl. This wholehearted thoroughness is beyond thinking.

Even when one is deeply concentrated and sitting in silence and stillness, karmic consciousness is alive and well. A sense of self is present in karmic consciousness, and it is accompanied by the delusion that this self is the director of thinking, the director of karmic activity. There may also be the delusion that the self is the director of concentration practice. But the self cannot perform thorough activity because when activity is thorough, there is no self or anything else in addition to the activity.

Our ancient teachers Hongzhi and Dogen were both deeply grateful and inspired by this story of Yaoshan's teaching of sitting in stillness. Hongzhi wrote verses in celebration of Yaoshan's teaching, and inspired by Hongzhi's verse, Dogen wrote this:

The pivotal activity of all buddhas,
The functioning pivot of all ancestors,
Present with thinking and with not-thinking,
Completed with and without interacting.

Present as thinking and not-thinking,
This presence is inherently intimate.
Completed as interacting and not-interacting,
This completion is actualized of itself.
This presence, inherently intimate, is never defiled.
This completion, actualized of itself, is never inclined or upright.
Intimacy that is never defiled,
Is liberated without relying on anything.
Actualization that is never inclined or upright,
Is genuine, actualized without intention.
The water is clear to the bottom: fish swim like fish.
The sky is vast, reaching into the heavens: birds fly like birds.[6]

This is the pivotal activity of all buddhas. When one sits and thinks thoroughly, in the fullness of thinking one realizes thinking is not-thinking and not-thinking is thinking. This reciprocal intimacy of thinking and not-thinking is expressed in Yaoshan's wholehearted sitting, which is beyond thinking. Yaoshan and the monk played with the word *thinking*. Shall we join them?

Beyond thinking is the great compassion of the buddhas. This great compassion is the room in which we thoroughly study our thinking and discover it is really not-thinking. Compassionately observing not-thinking, we discover that it is turning with thinking. Thus, we observe and enter into the pivotal activity of the buddhas and ancestors.

We can apply these teachings by compassionately observing the present moment of consciousness. Is there a sense of something that is called “I” or “me”? Are others also appearing in this consciousness? Are there landscapes filled with many kinds of living beings? This is a way to study egocentric consciousness. Studying in this way, we wholeheartedly study our thinking in the room of great compassion beyond thinking.

Thinking is the overall pattern of a moment of karmic consciousness. Using this definition of thinking, the conversation between Yaoshan and the monk can be rephrased as follows:

The monk asked, “What is the pattern of consciousness as you sit so immovably still?”

Yaoshan answered, “The pattern of consciousness is not the pattern of consciousness.”

Then the monk asked, “How is the pattern of consciousness not the pattern of consciousness?

And Yaoshan said, “It is beyond patterns of consciousness.”

To become free of our thinking, we need to study our thinking compassionately. Of course, sometimes we do not observe our thinking or the thinking of others with kindness. We can notice such things in the pattern of our thinking. Furthermore, we cannot become free of our thinking without having genuine conversation with good friends about how we are thinking. Just like the monk in conversation with Yaoshan.

The activity of great compassion is always present, although we might not be mindful or aware of it. However, sentient beings are often aware of the thinking that is going on in karmic consciousness. People often say to me, “I am always thinking,” and they usually say that with some discomfort with this seeming incessant thinking. It is auspicious to awakening when we are aware of thinking. Within this awareness, we have a chance to see that thinking is not thinking, that karma is not karma. Herein we have the opportunity to become free of thinking, which is being free of karma. We become free of the delusion that thinking or freedom belongs to us or somebody. This is an intimate and liberating vision of great compassion.

Right now, what is the pattern of karmic consciousness? Yaoshan said, "The pattern of consciousness is not the pattern of consciousness." The whole consciousness is viewing the whole consciousness. The whole consciousness is aware of its whole pattern. Our ancestors had such compassionate conversations about karmic consciousness.

We are called to engage in this conversation about karmic consciousness with great compassion. Great compassion means that no matter what is going on in our consciousness, we study it compassionately. Even if it is a pattern of hatred, we study it with compassion. Practicing compassion with karmic consciousness opens the mind of wisdom. Thus, we realize what buddha realizes. We do this by practicing compassion with whatever is appearing in consciousness. I pray that we study these patterns with compassion in conversation with others.

Being thorough in practicing Yangshan's instruction to reverse thought requires faith in this teaching, great determination, and courage. It also requires being upright, gentle, flexible, and harmonious in the midst of the thinking that goes on in the conscious mind. In upright thoroughness, our thought is spontaneously reversed without any additional effort. This practice realizes that the dynamic pivoting of thinking and not-thinking cannot be grasped. These teachings, given in the room of compassion by Yangshan, Yaoshan, and Dogen, offer immediate, intimate entry into the buddha way by reversing thought and taking a backward step into awakening. How wonderful that these buddha ancestors of distinctive lineages harmonize and enrich each other's teachings.

The compassionate bodhisattva Bodhidharma[7] taught his disciple Huike how to be wholeheartedly upright, inwardly and outwardly.

> *Bodhidharma said, "Outwardly allow all conditions to be still and inwardly no gasping or sighing. Thus, with a mind like a wall, enter the way."*
>
> *After some time, Huike said to Bodhidharma, "All conditions have come to rest."*
>
> *Bodhidharma said, "Doesn't that become extinction?"*
>
> *Huike said, "It does not become extinction."*
>
> *Bodhidharma said, "Prove it!"*
>
> *Huike said, "I am always clearly aware; therefore, no words reach it."*
>
> *Bodhidharma said, "This is the essence of mind realized by all buddhas. Doubt no more."*[8]

What is this "mind like a wall" that Bodhidharma is talking about? It is the wholehearted, upright mind of the compassionate bodhisattva that isn't busy adding or subtracting anything and welcomes everything just as it is. The thinking mind is functioning even after we have found our seat in silence and stillness. Our thinking is always based on past thinking, but in silence and stillness when nothing is added and nothing is subtracted, we are not bound by our thinking. This is Bodhidharma's instruction about how to enter the pivotal activity of all buddhas.

If we hear Bodhidharma's teaching of an upright mind like a wall and give ourselves to practicing this, it might take a long time to realize this compassionate mind. In some versions of the above story, Huike worked on this teaching together with Bodhidharma for seven years.

There is an art to relinquishing the outward and inward workings of our mind, but this art might not be easy to learn. In the process, we might lose our seat in silence and stillness. We could get excited, or we might resist just being where we are. One of the ways we get excited is to seek a method for reversing our thought. Many people try this way but, in the end, that is not relinquishing thought. Entering the buddha way is not accomplished by intellectual attempts to reverse thought.

If we wish to enter the buddha way by relinquishing thought, even if the mind does not stop going in its usual direction, we can still compassionately observe this state of affairs. We might observe that when the mind becomes active around internal and external objects of thought, we become an exhausted fish or a sluggish duck.

If we are able to clearly observe the energy inflation or deflation that occurs when the mind is activated around objects of thought, thought is reversed in that very moment. When we are free of all inflation and deflation, we enter the way of Bodhidharma. When there's no inflow or outflow around objects, we don't gain or lose anything. However, when we observe that the mind is involved in gain and loss, we are being called to compassionately practice confession and repentance.

In his "Universal Encouragement for the Ceremony of Sitting Meditation" ("Fukanzazengi"),[9] Dogen says, "Cast aside all involvements and cease all affairs. Do not think good or bad. Do not administer pros and cons. Cease all the movements of the conscious mind, the gauging of all thought and views. Have no designs on becoming a buddha." In other words, let go of all thought activity around all objects of awareness, even the vow to become buddha. Don't make that marvelous vow into another karmic trap. Part of realizing the vow to become buddha is to give up the idea of becoming buddha.

Bodhidharma is telling us not to get entangled in any ideas. Right off, flat out, let them go. This is the teaching of a mind like a wall. The instruction to consciousness is to stop doing anything about what is appearing and disappearing. The mind goes right ahead and does stuff, but then nothing is done about that doing. The function just goes on.

Allowing the natural functioning of consciousness is Yangshan's reversal of thought and Yaoshan's beyond thinking. We are being told to study with a mind like that. We are being taught to watch our thinking in a different way. Watching ourselves will be like watching somebody else, and watching somebody else will be like watching ourselves. Thus, we compassionately see through our thinking into the vast emptiness of all things.

This is our mind being like a wall. This is to cease being involved in the movements of the conscious mind. This mind is conscious of objects. Ceasing the movements means there is just awareness of objects: just awareness of walking, just awareness of listening, just awareness of touching, just awareness of smelling, just awareness of all kinds of concepts. And that's that. Things are still appearing and disappearing, but the mind is not jumping around the objects anymore. When we let our mind be like a wall, we have renounced worldly affairs and maintain our inheritance of the buddha way.

Whether we are in the confines of a monastery or in the wider world, we can get involved in worldly affairs. And whether we are in a monastery or in the wider world, we can give up worldly affairs. This renunciation is to turn around in our seat and enter the buddha way.

This is not just a theoretical turning. We turn right where we are. We are actually willing to be where we are, and we turn at this place. We can even walk in this place. When we walk, we just let the walking be the walking. While we are walking in this way, neither ahead of our walking nor behind our walking, we renounce worldly affairs. When we are concerned with the worldly affairs of gain and loss, we are ahead or behind ourselves.

Yangshan taught us to reverse our thinking and think of the thinking mind. This reversal of the mind is renouncing the mind. In renunciation we are no longer carried away by thoughts. Turn around and look at them. This is renouncing them. Study the place where we see things, say things, and do things. This is studying the thinking mind. Think of that mind. Think of that ability. Clearly observe. This is how to relinquish our mental activities. Relinquish them by thoroughly admitting them. Admit them to the end of them. Admit them at the beginning, at the middle, and at the end. Do nothing but that. Being this way is renunciation. No matter what the state is, whether we are an exhausted fish or a sluggish duck, or a celestial dragon or a wondrous crane, we can just clearly observe.

If we follow through completely on the teaching and training in reversing thought, we will experience the suchness of mind and object in which doors of liberation are open. Thus, we will be liberated from dualistic entanglements of subject and object. Through this meditation, we will realize that the world we see around us is not out there on its own, separate from our awareness. We will see that the world arises and ceases intimately together with the arising and ceasing of our body and mind. There will only be the intimacy of subject and object. Our obsessions and compulsions with objects will drop away, and we will enter Buddha's house.

But we have to have a mind like the destitute child in the parable who said yes to what was offered to him. He was offered work in the stables and then he was offered work in the house. Like the son when he was invited into his father's house, Yangshan's student said, "Yes!" and followed instructions that were given to him with faith and obedience. He attained entry into the house of Buddha that Yangshan calls the stage of faith. Both the son and the student have been turned by teachings and have now entered the house.

10

The Stage of Faith

YANGSHAN SAID TO THE MONK, "Are there so many things there?"

The monk said, "When I get here, I don't see any existence at all."

Then Yangshan said, "This is right for the stage of faith, but not yet right for the stage of person."

The monk received and faithfully followed Yangshan's instruction: "Reverse your thought to think of the thinking mind." He gave up concerns with objects in the environment and came into alignment with the instructions to reverse his thought and think of thinking. The student came to the teacher, paid respect, and followed the teacher's instructions with confidence. The monk's faith in the teaching was sincere; he gave himself completely to it.

The student gave himself completely to being the individual creature he thought he was and to studying thinking. At some point in his contemplation of the instruction, this monk was only thinking of the thinking mind, just awareness of awareness. In the depths of this awareness, the light of wisdom illuminated the conscious mind. He saw that awareness and all the things known by awareness do not fall neatly and definitively into the category of existence, nor do they fall into the category of nonexistence.

So when Yangshan asked, "Are there so many things there?" the disciple, looking directly into his awareness of thinking, found no objects. Therefore, he could honestly say, "When I get here, I don't see any existence at all." Then Yangshan said to him, "This is right for the stage of faith, but not yet right for the stage of person." Here he is confirming that the student has faithfully followed the teaching, and in doing so has awakened to his original nature. He has attained what Yangshan calls the stage of faith in which he doesn't see anything at all. The student has attained a mind undisturbed by objects. And because all the objects of the world that had previously disturbed his mind no longer exist as they did before, he says, "When I reach here, I don't see any existence at all."

This mind, undisturbed by objects, is what Yangshan called the stage of faith. This is a great attainment, but the student has not yet entered what Yangshan calls the stage of person. He has awakened to his original nature but is not yet ready to express it in his every action of body, speech, and mind. He has attained clarity in the midst of the objects in consciousness but has not yet reached the understanding of who he is. In the story, Yangshan subtly indicates his family business that the student needs to practice in order to realize the stage of person. This is like the son in the parable who has been invited to enter the house to learn the family business and learn about the treasures of the house. If and when the training in the family business (Yangshan's and the father's) comes to maturity, the student and the son will be ready for the revelations of the stage of person. I don't know if Yangshan's student accepted the instruction that Yangshan offered him—to go forward in his training and from there, seeing on his own. The son gladly accepted the invitation and gladly entered into training in the business of the great house.

This mind that the student monk attained, which is undisturbed by appearances of existence and nonexistence, is still only an initial realization of the deep intention of the teaching offered by Yangshan. This story speaks to the attainment of liberation by the monk and the next step, which he has not yet taken. Our life is more than karmic consciousness and the liberation from karmic consciousness. Our life also embraces and is embraced by the mind of perfect wisdom, which comprehends the relationship between karmic consciousness, the unconscious, and the body. Liberation from karmic consciousness is not the end of the story. Going beyond liberation, perfect wisdom reengages and liberates all living beings.

We don't know how long the monk contemplated Yangshan's instruction to "reverse your thought," but eventually the student did see through the thinking mind and glimpse the reality that runs through all things. Then he comes face-to-face with the teacher again and when Yangshan asks, "Are there so many things there?" the disciple can answer and does. But the answer, "I don't see any existence at all," although correct, doesn't go far enough. The student now needs to take another step and leap beyond this attainment to speak to the present meeting with the teacher person-to-person. But rather than giving Yangshan what he was asking for—a wholehearted expression of being a person—the student asks for more particular instruction: "Don't you have any other particular way of guidance?" The student had attained something really great, but he wasn't yet ready to let go of that and become a full-fledged member of Yangshan's family. The stage of person is not a stage of attainment. It is leaping beyond attainment and nonattainment.

This wonderful student seems stuck in the attainment of his original nature. Yangshan sees and acknowledges this situation and calls to him to leap beyond the stage of faith and meet face-to-face, person-to-person. In this way Yangshan indicates the vast horizons beyond inheriting the family business.

I imagine Yangshan saying to the disciple, "Okay, you've gone this far and now it's your turn to turn the teaching." But the student is not ready to meet this challenge and leap beyond his attainment into the wondrous and ordinary reality of being just a person. Instead of being the person he was right then and there, the person Yangshan was asking to meet, the student sidesteps this request and asks Yangshan for more instruction. The student says, "Don't you have any other particular way of guidance?" And Yangshan says, "To say that I have anything particular or not is not the point." The monk misses the point of responding as a person to Yangshan's question, "Are there so many things there?" Yangshan is saying that the student asking for more guidance misses the opportunity again; the opportunity to be and fully express the person he is right now.

The student's mind had turned and entered, but after entering, the student seemed to wallow in being free of appearances of existence and nonexistence. He made a nest in the attainment and missed the opportunity to walk forward onto the stage of person. The student saw the emptiness of all appearances, but then he made this emptiness into a thing. In doing so, he temporarily missed the opportunity to realize who he really was in this meeting with the teacher person-to-person. Yangshan graciously did *not* give the student further instructions on how to be a person. He leaves that for the student to discover on his own.

So the student became free but didn't go far enough to offer some creative expression of this newfound freedom. While he did say, "When I get here, I don't see any existence at all," he could have gone beyond that to say, "And yet, I'm filled with gratitude for your kindness and compassion. Is there anything I can do to help you with your work?" The student was graciously given a delicious meal and was being asked to return the favor, but rather than doing so, he asked for more food.

This is like the time in the parable when the father comes to the son and says, "You are just like a son to me," meaning "You and I are no different." The son is happy to hear this, but he doesn't ask, "What do you mean by that? Am I like a son, or am I actually your son?" At this point, the son missed his chance to really meet his father, just like the monk missed his opportunity to return the favor to Yangshan.

Yangshan's instruction to the student to reverse his thinking may be seen as appropriate for one who has done considerable training in the practices of generosity, ethics, patience, diligence, and concentration in the midst of the dung of karmic consciousness. When the student understands and follows the instruction, the teacher actually does give further, particular guidance, saying, "This is right for the stage of faith, but not yet right for the stage of person."

When the student asks for more particular guidance, Yangshan says, "To say that I have anything particular or not misses the point." I can imagine Yangshan thinking, "I already *gave* you particular guidance, my dear." Now, Yangshan is not giving the student, or us, anything additional to look at. He is encouraging us to look more deeply into the particular that he has already given and discover the universal riches of our original nature.

The teacher meets and uses everything that comes as an opportunity for teaching. He could be seeing anything—a wall, perhaps a shadow on the wall—or hearing the sound of rain. When the truth is realized, we meet and use whatever comes as an opportunity to practice the buddhas' family business. Then everything that comes to us is buddhadharma. This mature response depends on buddhadharma and expresses buddhadharma; it *is* buddhadharma. This is what Yangshan is pointing to with the phrase "the stage of person."

There is no particular dharma by which authentic awakening is realized. Awakening uses whatever comes without depending on anything. It uses whatever comes without clinging or rejecting. Something comes, the teaching occurs, and we respond without having or not having anything. So Yangshan says, "To say that I have anything particular or not, would not be accurate." But then ironically, after Yangshan says this, he gives the monk some particular guidance, some details about what the monk has attained and what he has not attained.

At the same time that we receive particular, perceptible guidance, we are also receiving imperceptible universal guidance, but we need to open to and exhaustively study the particular to realize the universal. This is a middle way wherein universal and particular are mutually included without abiding in either.

In late December of 1969, I met Suzuki Roshi in the hall of Zen Center and reminded him that I would soon be going to Tassajara for the winter practice period. He told me that he would like me to study chanting with the visiting teacher who was going to lead the practice period. He extended his hand, and I received it. We shook hands. At that time, I felt great warmth coming from his hand, and I was also struck with the realization that the warmth I felt at that time had always been there. The particular warmth of his handshake opened the door to universal warmth, which I had never touched before.

The particular and the universal are a double dharma door. Commenting on the intense interactions of this story about the Middle Way, Wansong said, "[Yangshan] shoots through the double gate." Yangshan doesn't fall into the perceptible side of the gate, nor does he fall into the imperceptible side of the gate. He just stands upright at the threshold where they meet. He doesn't abide in having particular guidance, nor does he abide in not having particular guidance. He uses both freely. He goes right straight through.

Centuries after Yangshan, Dogen Zenji offered this poem in celebration of the middle way that passes freely through ever-changing particular phenomena and never-changing universal principle.

Always
since these flowers are invariably
blooming
in my home village.
the colors do not change
although spring passes[1]

Yangshan's student did not come as far as the son did at the end of the parable. His understanding is right for the stage of faith, but it is not yet mature. Through his work in the house, the destitute son learned to care for the particular treasures of the family. In this process, the universal jewels of his original family will be revealed to him. At the end of the parable, the destitute child, through his long and faithful practice, will not only attain his inheritance; he will also understand that it had always been his. However, Zen practice lets go of all such attainments.

11

The Three Mysteries

AT THE END OF THE STORY OF YANGSHAN AND THE MONK, Yangshan seemed at first to refrain from giving his student further guidance, but then he changed his mind and gave a little more. When the student expressed his insight, Yangshan said, "Based on your insight, you only get one mystery—you can take the seat and wear the robe. After this, see on your own."

We don't really know how the monk responded to Yangshan's final gift. What follows in this chapter imagines a path of practice to bring the monk's training to completion so that he could fully receive his entire inheritance.

The first mystery comes in the turning of mind and in realizing the emptiness of awareness itself. It comes in seeing that all things are ambiguous and free of any basis for apprehension. This initial understanding of the emptiness of conventional reality is the first mystery. Here one attains disentanglement from objects of awareness.

When we are free from such entanglement, we may feel some relief from suffering and be satisfied. This relief and satisfaction are both a blessing and a challenge. We must be careful of this first mystery. Otherwise, we may miss the wild, spontaneous, creative activity of our life. Like the student, when we first become disentangled from the objects that our body and mind have constructed and projected onto reality, we may say that we can't find any existence at all. We can't find any basis for apprehending anything. When something appears to definitively exist, it seems that we can get hold of it. And vice versa, when we seem to get ahold of something, it seems to exist. It seems to be substantial and unambiguous.

Our ordinary consciousness imagines objects that appear to exist on their own. If it didn't do that, it would be very difficult to participate in ordinary society. Projecting apparently substantial objects onto reality is part of living in the human world. Our body and mind are born learning to do this. When we have learned this and understand it, we may begin the work of unlearning it.

This unlearning is mysterious because we are still here, living with everyone and everything as usual, seeing them and hearing them, and yet mysteriously, we can't find them existing on their own after all. Now we understand that the objects we see and hear are mental constructions projected onto the reality of our life. This unlearning, this disentanglement, is the first mystery, which Yangshan's student attained.

The next two mysteries go beyond this initial realization. The student got stuck in the first mystery and had not yet entered the other two more subtle mysteries, wherein we fully and freely inhabit our original nature. The student is simply disentangled, detached from objects of awareness. He experienced a preliminary, authentic detachment but had not yet experienced detachment from that detachment. In other words, the student was stuck in the freedom of this detachment and was not yet able to let go of the attainment of detachment and use attachment to demonstrate the bodhisattva way. For this, he needs further study of the mysteries.

The second mystery is going beyond the freedom of detachment. This means thoroughly studying this freedom from attachment and realizing its limitations. Compassion was involved in the way Yangshan worked with the monk to realize the first mystery. Within vast space of the second mystery, there is freedom from the freedom of detachment. But within this spacious mystery, compassion calls and is called to reengage in the world of attachment again in new ways. The second mystery is motivation for going further and entering the third mystery.

Once we have realized the limits of the freedom from detachment of the second mystery, we are drawn into the third mystery: letting go of the disentanglement from detachment. It is liberating to be entangled when we are thoroughly aware of how entangled we are and how entanglement works. When we get thoroughly entangled in objects and study the entanglement, we will naturally be led again to realizing the emptiness of awareness and its objects.

In this third mystery, one is able to be creative, to look and act as if one were grasping things as though they were substantial objects. In other words, one is willing to be completely ordinary. Maybe one could even enjoy getting entangled in objects again as a work of art. It is liberating to be entangled when we are thoroughly aware of how entangled we are and how entanglement works. If we have a seat, we can give the seat away. We can offer the seat to someone else. We can invite them to sit down and talk, and the ensuing conversation generously and creatively allows both entanglement and freedom. In this conversation, we are meeting our friends and entering into the practice of the second mystery with them. We are meeting them wherever they are and talking with them. We are asking something of each other, and we are listening to each other. In such a conversation, we become like Yangshan.

The third mystery emerges spontaneously from the wholehearted conversations of the second mystery. The third mystery is to be thoroughly creative with attachment and detachment. In this situation, creativity is so complete that it is free of the idea of anybody being creative. We play freely. Entanglement drops away along with the idea of disentanglement. The third mystery is to be free of entanglement and disentanglement and to use both or neither within this subtle communion.

In the following story, the Zen teacher Tetsugyu demonstrates this transcendent working of intimate conversation.

> *Tetsugyu (Iron Bull) was serving tea to Lord Sendai in a precious antique bowl that the warlord had given him. The warlord also invited Tetsugyu's dharma brother Cho-on (Tidal Sound) to have tea with him. As the teabowl was placed on the tatami mat before them, and they were appreciating its beauty, Cho-on suddenly reached out with the ceremonial baton he was carrying and smashed it.*
>
> *"Now look at the authentic teabowl that exists before birth," he said.*

Tetsugyu was aghast, but Lord Sendai calmly said, "I gave you that teabowl. Now please give it back to me. But first have it glued back together and have a box made to hold it. On the cover of the box, please write the name 'Authentic Teabowl before Birth.'"

Lord Sendai said he would cherish it and pass the bowl on to his descendants.[1]

Cho-on used Tetsugyu's attachment to the form of the teabowl to demonstrate the deep vitality of the teabowl. Lord Sendai appreciated this. He wanted to celebrate this for future generations and went beyond the breaking of the form.

Working with the subtleties of these three mysteries, our body and mind become intimate with the bodies and minds of others. A person may appear to be creative, but the form of that creativity might reveal some subtle form of clinging. The three mysteries are a way of talking about the thorough pivoting of attachment and awakening. Realizing the three mysteries is realizing how enlightenment includes delusion and delusion includes enlightenment. They are the vast ongoing and open-ended activity of our life, wherein there is no camping out in either bondage or freedom.

The three mysteries are dynamically present in our original nature. Our original nature, our intimacy with all beings, embraces all three mysteries. In realizing the mysteries, we realize who and what we really are together with all beings. These three mysteries are present in our wandering away, and they are present in our homecoming. They are present in forgetting, and they are there in remembering.

In the *Lotus Sutra*, in a chapter called "Dharma Teacher," the Buddha speaks of teaching the sutra after he is gone. He says to the bodhisattva Medicine King,

> "Medicine King, after the extinction of the Tathagata,[2] if there are good sons or good daughters who want to teach this *Dharma Flower Sutra* for the four groups,[3] how should they teach it? Such good sons or good daughters should enter the room of the Tathagata, put on the robe of the Tathagata, sit on the seat of the Tathagata, and then teach this sutra everywhere for the four groups.
>
> "To enter the room of the Tathagata is to have great compassion for all living beings. To wear the robe of the Tathagata is to be gentle and patient. To sit on the seat of the Tathagata is to contemplate the emptiness of all things. One should dwell in peace with all three and then, never becoming lazy or careless, teach this *Dharma Flower Sutra* everywhere to bodhisattvas and the four groups."[4]

The room of the Tathagata is the heart of great compassion for all living beings. The robe of the Tathagata is the mind of gentleness and flexibility and patience. The seat of the Tathagata is the emptiness of all phenomena. Entering the room of the Tathagatha, wearing the robe of the Tathagatha, and sitting on the seat of the Tathagatha, we are ready to teach the dharma.

In our story, when Yangshan said to his student, "Based on your insight . . . you can take the seat and wear the robe," he opened the doors of buddha's room of great compassion, and the upright student entered. The student wore the robe of the Tathagata and sat on the seat of the Tathagata, and this Yangshan confirmed. But Yangshan didn't mention the room of the Tathagata. Perhaps this was because while the student was sitting on buddha's seat and wearing buddha's robe, saying, "When I get here, I don't see any existence at all," he was not reopening the doors of great compassion and welcoming all beings to enter.

To receive the dharma, we need to enter the room of great compassion. We need to enter this dharma heart. We need to don the mind of gentleness and patience, which is buddha's robe. Then we need to sit on the seat of emptiness, the ultimate truth of all things. Wearing buddha's robe and sitting on the seat of ultimate truth in buddha's room, we are ready to open the doors and teach the dharma.

In Zen practice, before we first put on buddha's robe in the morning, we chant the following verse:

Great is the robe of liberation!
A field far beyond form and emptiness
Wearing the Tathagata's teaching
Saving all beings.[5]

Wearing the robe of gentleness and patience, we sit on the seat of ultimate truth and offer the heart of great compassion. Thus, we invite all living beings to enter the room, put on the robe, and sit next to us on the Tathagata's seat of ultimate truth. Then we, all together, may join the process of teaching the dharma, freeing all beings so that they may live in peace.

The student came forward to meet Yangshan face-to-face. The student entered Yangshan's room of great compassion.

Receiving and practicing Yangshan's instructions, the student donned the robe and ascended the seat. But he was not ready to show us how to descend from the seat and invite all beings to enter the room to practice and enjoy the inconceivable buddhadharma together. Yangshan called the monk to explore practices that would bring him to maturity, but the story does not tell us if he was able to follow through.

At the moment we enter the room of great compassion, Buddha is there to meet us. All beings are there to meet us. When we sit at our place in the room, wrapped in the teaching, by the power of great compassion, we let go of the ultimate truth of emptiness and reenter the world of form and feeling. We join hands with all beings and practice creatively together with them. This creativity is an opportunity for compassion, and compassion is an opportunity for creativity. When people come to meet us in this room, we may offer them a seat and some water or tea, and perhaps a question. Yangshan's disciple didn't seem ready to make such an offering, and his unreadiness is not right for the stage of person.

In the room of the Tathagatha, sitting on the Tathagata's seat, wearing the Tathagata's robe, we use whatever comes as an opportunity for our practice because we are not attached to any particular form of practice. We may have something particular to offer, and we can use whatever comes because of nonattachment. The room, the robe, and the seat will conspire with us to offer an appropriate response. In this way, the buddhadharma is taught and practiced. Because it doesn't abide in being this way, or being not this way, or being both this way *and* not this way, there is the opportunity for the appropriate, compassionate response to arise.

The student entered Yangshan's room, and Yangshan showed the student around. The student received Yangshan's gifts and enjoyed the great compassion of the room. The student received buddha's robe and practiced gently and patiently. He realized the teachings to the point that he couldn't see any existence at all. But when the student expressed his understanding, this understanding did not allow all living beings to enter. He was not yet able to fully accept the inheritance of Yangshan's teaching.

So Yangshan says, "From now on, see on your own." In other words, he is telling the monk that he has more work to do. It's up to him to learn how to open the doors of the Tathagata's room and welcome beings into the family business. He is telling the monk, and us, to go beyond trying to get the dharma from somebody else and to let it flow out of your own breast and cover the whole world.

In celebrating the monk's understanding and showing its limits, National Teacher Deshao[6] offered the following verse comment on this story:

Crossing the summit of the mystic peak,
It's not the human world;
Outside the mind there are no things—
Filling the eyes are blue mountains[7]

The first three lines of the poem could describe the fruits of the stage of faith, which Yangshan's student attained. The last line points to going beyond the stage of faith to what was not realized, the stage of person. The monk sees that outside the mind there are no things but does not yet allow the eyes to be filled with the blue mountains, the great earth, and all living beings and thus to enter the stage of person. To fully inherit the dharma and go on to free all beings so they may live in peace, we need to not only climb to the summit of the mystic peak and enter the room of Buddha's compassion. We must also descend from the heights and invite all beings to enter the room and walk through the mountains and valleys of birth and death together with us. I pray that we may walk together with all beings right now.

12

Realizing the Stage of Person

AT THE END OF THE PARABLE, the destitute child finally realizes his original nature, who he is and always has been. Through a long process of wandering away in confusion, returning home, being trained in shoveling dung in his father's stables, and becoming intimate with many other facets of the family business, he has become confident and clear. It is revealed to him that he is the legitimate heir and successor of a great family. The final realization of the destitute child, awakening to the truth of who he is, is what Yangshan refers to as the stage of person.

What Yangshan refers to as the stage of person is awakening to the ambiguity and emptiness of being a person. This is seeing that we are a person, and we are otherwise. The great and challenging work of realizing the mystery of who and what we really are is at the heart of Zen training. In the following stories about our ancestor Dongshan, we begin our exploration of the ambiguity of being a person.

After studying intimately with his teacher, Yunyan (Cloud Cliff), for a long time, Dongshan was ripe and ready to leave.

Just before departing, he asked, "After a hundred years, if someone asked me how I would portray your teaching, what should I say?"

Yunyan said, "Just this person."

Dongshan wondered what the teacher meant. And Yunyan said, "Having accepted responsibility for this great matter, you must be very careful."

Dongshan continued to wonder about what Yunyan said.

Later, after walking for a long time, as he was crossing a river Dongshan saw his reflection in the water and awoke to the meaning of Yunyan's words.[1]

Having accepted the responsibility of this great dharma inheritance, Dongshan left his teacher. He went on a pilgrimage and contemplated his teacher's final instruction with each step. He walked a long way and, upon seeing his reflection in the water as he was crossing a river, he finally realized "just this person" and he composed the following verse.

Earnestly avoid seeking without,
Lest it recede far from you.
Today I am walking alone,
Yet everywhere I meet him.
He is now no other than myself,
But I am not now him.
It must be understood in this way
In order to merge with suchness.[2]

Then he devoted his life to transmitting "just this person" to everyone and everything he met. Together with his students, he founded a monastery at a place called Dongshan (Cave Mountain), so we call him Dongshan. This monastery is just a few hundred yards from the place in the stream where he awoke. Dongshan and his community settled into their work. They continued to study and practice together intimately.

I imagine that after Dongshan awoke to his original nature while crossing the stream, he continued to live near that place of awakening and to enjoy the fruits of realizing the teaching of "just this person." He couldn't help but share this realization with everyone he met. He met people, and they met him. In this way, he transcended and transmitted the inheritance and welcomed the next generation into the family business.

Years ago, when I visited Dongshan's monastery, I also stood in that stream of awakening. Standing there in the stream, one of the pilgrims I was traveling with said that this place seemed more like the stream in our home monastery of Tassajara than any other place we had visited in China, and I agreed with her.

There was a bridge nearby on which there was an inscription in Chinese that said, "Where he encountered it." I asked a Chinese Buddhist scholar who was with us how far the spot where we were standing was from Dongshan's teacher's temple. He said it was about one hundred and fifty miles. I imagine Dongshan walking one hundred and fifty miles and finally, with the help of his reflection in the water, realizing the importance of "just this person is not just this person." He said, " Now he is no other than myself, but I am not now him." He saw that this person was no other than himself and that this person was also otherwise. This person includes all others and is included in all others.

In the same time period as Dongshan, there was a monk named Jinhua Juzhi who was also struggling to realize who he truly was.[3] He lived and practiced in a hut on Mount Tiantai.

> *One night, a nun named Shiji (Reality) arrived at Juzhi's hut to pay him a visit. Wearing her rain hat and carrying a staff in her hand, she entered the hut. She walked around him three times, stood in front of him without removing her hat as would have been usual, and said, "If you can speak, I'll take off my hat."*
>
> *She said this three times, but Juzhi couldn't speak. So, Reality started to go away. Juzhi called out, "It's getting late. Just stay the night." Reality said, "If you can speak, I'll stay." Again, Juzhi could not respond and so the nun named Reality left.*
>
> *Then, after Reality had gone, Juzhi lamented to himself, "Although I have the body of a man, I don't have the spirit of a man. Maybe it would be better if I left this hut and went on a pilgrimage to find a teacher."*[4]

Reading this story, we might really wonder what was actually going on in their meeting. It seems as though they had not met before. And it seems really unusual that a nun would visit a monk that she didn't know in his private dwelling in the nighttime and express herself so dramatically and openly. There are many possible interpretations about what might have been going on between them. What does seem clear is that Juzhi was challenged by her powerful presence and unable to respond to her request that he fully express himself. He wasn't able to be "just this person" with her.

Then, as Juzhi was about to leave his hut and go off on pilgrimage to study, a mountain spirit came to him and said, "You don't need to leave this mountain. A great bodhisattva will come in the flesh and demonstrate the dharma for you."

And, amazingly, within ten days, a bodhisattva named Tianlong (Celestial Dragon) arrived at his hut. Juzhi formally welcomed and respectfully prostrated to him. He then recounted what had happened previously. Tianlong simply raised one finger and pointed at him, whereupon Juzhi realized the great awakening.[5]

Tianlong transmitted "just this person" by raising one finger, and Juzhi awakened and inherited it. From that time on, whenever anyone asked him for teaching, Juzhi just raised one finger. He offered no other teaching throughout his illustrious teaching career. When he was about to die, he said to the monks that he had attained Tianlong's teaching of one finger but that, in his entire life, he still had not exhausted it. When he had finished saying this, he passed away. And since he didn't exhaust it, the mystery of one finger is still available for us to contemplate and realize. After this meeting with his teacher, Juzhi became one of the most iconic teachers of the Zen tradition. He became just this person.

The historical records on the life of Juzhi are scant. We don't know the dates of his birth and death, but his simple, clear teaching has been celebrated by many teachers and students for more than a thousand years. Like Juzhi, we have not exhausted our exploration of this teaching of one finger, and we never will. But we may aspire to practice it.

This teaching of one finger was also transmitted by Suzuki Roshi. Commenting on this story, Suzuki Roshi asked us, "What do you think this one finger is?" Once, as he was transmitting it to us, he was uncharacteristically challenging. He said something like, "Most of you don't have the conviction of this one finger. I should tell you to go away!" "Go away" means "come back." Come back when you have the confidence to practice this one-finger teaching. That is to say, "Come back and meet me when you have confidence in being 'just this person,' whatever that is." In this way, Suzuki Roshi helps us keep Juzhi and his teaching alive.

Like Suzuki Roshi I ask, "What do you think this one finger is?" The dharma body of awakening is free of all elaboration. The teacher Juzhi always taught the dharma by just raising one finger. Do you think it's ironic that now I am elaborating on this great teaching, which is free of elaboration? Does this question encourage you to realize the one finger of no elaboration? Or does it tempt you to wander away into elaboration? The oceans of elaborations of the Zen school are all included within this one finger of no elaboration. Within "just this person" is the great joke of the One Finger of Ten Million.

There is another parable offered in the *Lotus Sutra* that resonates for me with the story about the destitute child and illuminates another nuance in the process of transmitting the blessings of buddha's family. In this second parable, a poor person visited a wealthy friend and was served wine. The guest became drunk and fell asleep. His generous host was suddenly called away to take care of some urgent business. While the guest was sleeping, the host sewed a priceless pearl into the lining of the guest's robe and then went away. Later the guest woke up and left, not knowing about the treasure sewn into the robe. This poor person traveled to another place and continued to encounter great difficulty in earning enough to provide food and other basic needs. Eventually by chance, he ran into the host again. Seeing and hearing about this person's difficulties, the wealthy benefactor scolded the poor friend and explained that while the guest was sleeping, a pearl had been sewn into his robe. The benefactor called the poor friend a fool for not discovering and using the treasure that was given to him.

On the path of awakening, we sincerely aspire to realize the truth. Even though it is always being intimately transmitted to us right where we are, we often look for it in some other time or place. We might imagine that it's something other than our daily life. And yet, it cannot be the slightest bit different from our present life. Although it is transmitted to us, it is not necessarily something we recognize. Realization is not an object of recognition. Realization is who we already are. The parable illuminates this great irony.

Our compassionate ancestor Shunryu Suzuki devoted his life to transmitting the dharma jewel to us. The following story also illustrates the situation described in the parable.

One day Suzuki Roshi said to me, "I want to give you some teachings on the "Sandokai" ("The Harmony of Difference and Equality"), but I want to say some things that may not be appropriate to give to the whole community in the Buddha Hall."

Not long after that, he invited me to his *dokusan* (private interview) room. He called me out of my diligent practice in the stables and invited me into his room to teach me some of the subtleties of the family business. We sat cross-legged, wearing our priest robes. Meeting me face-to-face, he kindly offered his teaching. After he started, I was very embarrassed by feeling drowsy. Was I drowsed by the fume of the dharma? I don't think I was completely asleep. I was awake enough to feel extremely embarrassed about my drowsiness. My kind and generous teacher was giving me this precious opportunity to hear the dharma, and I was not awake for it. I was on the verge of falling asleep. How outrageous! And amazing! How intimate! And today, half a century later, I am still embarrassed and amazed that such a thing happened. I really don't remember anything of what he said. But I very clearly remember that we were there together and knew this was a precious moment, and I was having a very hard time staying awake. Nonetheless, he just kept giving me the teaching. He didn't say, "How dare you sleep right in front of me like this!" and conclude the talk; he did not. He was so patient with me. He just went on and on pouring the dharma over me and into me. He sewed jewels into my robes when I was asleep. I don't know what he said, but I do remember his patience and generosity and those moments with him for which I am deeply grateful.

In commenting on the parable of the jewel sewn into the robe, our great ancestor Dogen made a rather startling comment. He said something like, "When the dharma is transmitted to us, we are invariably drunk." Maybe my sleepiness allowed the jewel to be sewn into my robes. But I still feel embarrassed about it. Suzuki Roshi secretly gave me a jewel while we were sitting together, and I'm sharing it with you now although I still haven't fully comprehended it.

Before I asked to be ordained as a priest, I was intending to receive lay bodhisattva precepts. As part of that process, I was sewing a traditional Buddhist robe (*rakusu*). During the lengthy period of sewing, I asked Suzuki Roshi to ordain me as a priest. He agreed to do so. I am embarrassed to confess that in the time leading up to priest ordination, I lost track of the robe that I was sewing for lay ordination. Sometime after I was ordained as a priest, I found the robe and finished sewing it. I then offered it to Suzuki Roshi with a respectful request that he inscribe the back of the robe with calligraphy. He did so and gave it back to me. At that time, I could read that the calligraphy had something to do with the image of a jewel under a robe, but I didn't understand all of the calligraphy, and I did not ask Suzuki Roshi to translate it.

Recently, as I thought about the parable of the jewel hidden in the robe, I thought of that calligraphy again, and I got some help in translating it more thoroughly. And lo and behold, I found that the calligraphy was referring to the parable in the *Lotus Sutra* about a good friend secretly sewing a jewel into his poor friend's robe. Here is the translation of what Suzuki Roshi wrote on the back of the robe:

The jewels hidden in the back of the robe
Are not known by scholars
Who uselessly count
The words of Buddhist scriptures.

The ancient teacher Longtan Chongxin (Dragon Pond Respectful Faith)[6] studied with and eventually became a successor of the teacher Tianhuang Daowu.[7] Daowu sewed jewels into

Chongxin's robes unbeknownst to him. When Chongxin became a teacher, he in turn sewed jewels into the robes of his students. His family's business was making and selling tea cakes. As a boy, Chongxin delivered them all around. Apparently, the teacher Daowu lived in his neighborhood.

Each day, Chongxin would present ten cakes as an offering to Daowu.

Each time Daowu would leave one cake saying, "This is for the sake of your descendants."

One day, the boy said, "I take cakes everywhere. So why do you leave one for me? Does it have any special meaning?"

Daowu said, "You bring the cakes everywhere. So what harm is there to return one to you?"

At these words, the boy grasped the deeper meaning. Because of this, he left home to study with Daowu.

After some time Daowu said, "Previously you were respectful to virtue and goodness, and now you place your faith in what I say, so you'll be named Chongxin [Respect Faith]." Thereafter, Chongxin remained close to Daowu as his attendant.

One day Chongxin asked Zen Master Daowu, "Since I've come here, you've never taught me about essential mind."

Daowu said, "Since you've come here, I've never instructed you about anything other than the essence of mind.

Chongxin said, "How have you pointed it out?"

And Daowu said, "When you bring me tea, I receive the tea for you. When you bring food to me, I receive it for you. When you do prostrations to me, I bow my head. In all this, where have I not given instruction about your essential mind?"

Chongxin bowed his head for a long time.

Daowu said, "Look at it directly. If you think about it, you will miss it."

Hearing these words, Chongxin woke up. Chongxin then asked Daowu, "How does one uphold this?"

Daowu said, "Live in an unfettered way, in accord with circumstances. Give yourself to everyday mind for there is nothing to be realized outside of this."[8]

In this story Chongxin seems to be longing for a deep teaching about the essence of mind. The teacher skillfully responded to help him realize the teaching, but the student didn't understand. After some time, the student says, "You never give me any deep teaching." Then the teacher says, "What? Have I not been teaching you that?" It's a story about a student looking for the jewels that the teacher has already given to him. The student says, "Will you give me a jewel??" The teacher says, "I've been giving you jewels all along. Where were you? Didn't you see me sharing the essence of mind with you in all of our daily interactions?"

Every day all day long, Daowu sewed jewels into his disciple's robes, but the disciple was not aware of the transmission. Finally, through Daowu's great kindness and compassion, Chongxin discovered the hidden jewels. Later, Chongxin (Respectful Faith) became the abbot of Longtan (Dragon Pond) Monastery and was thereafter referred to by the name Dragon Pond.

By the force of imagination, I offer you the following fantasy: It is the golden age of Zen, and Zen monks and nuns, laymen and laywomen wandered around in the mountains visiting various teachers to study the dharma. After Dragon

Pond became abbot of this monastery, he encouraged his dharma friends and family to set up tea shops in the mountains and valleys around the monastery as places to intercept potential Zen masters and transmit the family jewels to them. If a likely candidate showed up, the proprietor would test their understanding and offer some appropriate response. Sometimes the teaching could be completed on the spot. The jewels could be transmitted and discovered, and the heir to the jewels could share the wealth with all beings. If the transmission was incomplete, the proprietor would recommend that the future buddha go to see Dragon Pond, who might be able to finish the job.

There was at that time an esteemed scholar-monk named Deshan Xuanjian (Virtue Mountain Proclamation Mirror) whose family name was Zhou.[9] He was a brilliant exponent of the *Diamond Sutra of Perfect Wisdom*, so he was nicknamed Diamond Zhou. Although he was a person of great learning, it seems that his understanding was somewhat academic and immature. He was ripe to fall into Dragon Pond's tea-shop trap.

> *[W]hen Deshan heard that the Southern School of Zen was flourishing, he railed against it, saying, "Those who leave home may study the great meaning of Buddhism for a thousand kalpas and spend a further ten thousand kalpas performing detailed Buddhist practices, yet they still won't become a buddha. How dare those Southern Devils say that just by pointing at the human mind, one can see self-nature and attain buddhahood. I'll go drag them from their caves and exterminate their ilk and thus repay the kindness of Buddha."*

With copies of the Qinglong commentaries on his back, Deshan set out from Min. As he traveled on the road in Liyang, he came upon an old woman selling dim sum. Stopping to rest, Deshan bought a small meal.

The old woman pointed at his bundle and asked, "What are those books?"

Deshan said, "They are the Qinglong commentaries."

The old woman said, "What sutra do they expound on?"

Deshan said, "The Diamond Sutra."

Then the old woman said, "I have a question for you. If you answer it right, I'll donate the dumpling to you. If you can't answer, then you must go elsewhere. In the Diamond Sutra *it says, 'The bygone mind can't be attained. The present mind can't be attained. The future mind can't be attained.' I want to know, monk, what mind are you revealing right now?"*

Deshan was speechless.[10]

The old woman kindly directed him to see Dragon Pond. When Deshan arrived at Dragon Pond monastery, he went to the main hall. When Dragon Pond saw him coming, he stepped behind a screen.

Entering the hall Deshan said, "I've long heard of Dragon Pond, but arriving here I don't see a pond or a dragon."

Then Dragon Pond stepped out from behind the screen and said, "So now you have really seen the dragon and the pond." Deshan did not speak, but he stood in attendance upon the teacher.

As the evening wore on, Dragon Pond said, "It's getting late. You should go now."

Stepping outside the hall, Deshan said, "It's dark out here."

> *Dragon Pond then lit a paper lantern and brought it to Deshan. Just as Deshan received the lantern, Dragon Pond blew it out. And when the light went out, Deshan was enlightened, and he bowed deeply.*[11]

In this way, Deshan became Dragon Pond's successor. By the kindness of the tea lady and Dragon Pond, Deshan discovered the family jewels of Zen. When the lights went out, he entered the depths of the darkness in which the light was revealed. Meeting with Dragon Pond in this way, they harmonized darkness and light, sameness and difference, one and many. Flowing from this great harmony, Dragon Pond dramatically predicted that Deshan's teaching would cover the whole earth.

Deshan went on from Dragon Pond, and his teachings spread just as Dragon Pond predicted. Deshan nurtured and midwifed authentic successors. Two of the greatest were Xuefeng Yicun (Snow Peak) and Yantou Quanhuo (Cliff Top), who not only studied with Deshan, they also studied with each other.[12] They worked together closely, person-to-person and face-to-face, in the family business of realizing authentic awakening.

Xuefeng was a paragon of intense and sincere practice. He expressed his devotion in serving various communities as a cook, and he is also often referred to as an exemplar of wholehearted devotion to sitting meditation. They say that Xuefeng wore out nine meditation cushions. Many diligent Zen students have not even worn out one.

Yantou's relationship with his teacher Deshan was often rambunctious. This could also be said about his relationship with his dharma brother Xuefeng. Yantou was, as we say, a person who was very much himself. In this way, he was also *ten-shin*, or naturally real. Unlike his dharma brother, he had gotten over seeking outside of himself. As we will see later, Yantou also kindly taught Xuefeng how to give up searching outside.

After his awakening while crossing the stream, Dongshan expressed verses where he earnestly encouraged us to give up seeking outside ourselves. We, and all of our buddha ancestors, need this teaching. One of our ancestors who especially needed this encouragement was Xuefeng. He spent years diligently going against what Dongshan expressed. He searched for "just this person" outside himself.

> *When Xuefeng was traveling with his dharma brother Yantou on Tortoise Mountain in Li province, they were temporarily stuck at an inn during a snowstorm. Yantou spent the entire day sleeping. Xuefeng spent the entire day sitting in Zen meditation.*[13]

Xuefeng scolded Yantou for his sleeping, and Yantou encouraged him to relax, but Xuefeng couldn't.

> *Xuefeng said, "I'm truly anxious."*
>
> *Yantou said, "If that is really so, then reveal your understanding, and where it is correct, I'll confirm it for you. Where it's incorrect, I'll root it out."*
>
> *Xuefeng said, "When I first went to Yanguan's place,*[14] *I heard him expound on emptiness and form. At that time, I found an entrance."*
>
> *Yantou said, "For the next thirty years, don't speak of this matter again."*

Touched by Xuefeng's sadness and anxiety, the formerly slumbering giant Yantou sits up, invites Xuefeng to reveal his understanding, and offers to confirm where it is correct and root out where it is incorrect. Then Xuefeng recounts three experiences that have led to his understanding. Each time Yantou fiercely responds to Xuefeng's incomplete understanding. Xuefeng says he first "found an entrance" after hearing Yanguan expound on emptiness and form. Like Yangshan's student, Xuefeng gained entrance into the stage of faith, but Yantou's response—"Don't speak of this matter again"—sets backward-leaning Xuefeng upright. From now on, let's not wallow in such wonders from the past lest we fall into poverty in the present and the future.

> *Then Xuefeng said, "And then I saw Dongshan's poem that said, 'Avoid seeking elsewhere, for that's far from the Self, now I travel alone, everywhere I meet it, now it's exactly me, now I'm not it.'"*
>
> *Yantou said, "If that's so, you'll never save yourself."*

Next, Xuefeng tells Yantou that he had insight when he heard Dongshan's poem, "Avoid seeking elsewhere. . . ." Again, Yantou asks him for his understanding, here and now, but Xuefeng only offers insights from the past. So, Yantou says that he will not be free of his anxiety if he proceeds in this way. How funny that only a great Zen student like Xuefeng could be so dense and not see that, ironically, he was looking elsewhere to reveal his insight into Dongshan's admonition to "avoid seeking elsewhere."

Only a child of boundless wealth could fall into such profound poverty. Xuefeng's self-inflicted wounds were so deep that his recovery from them turned out to have mythic proportions, which we celebrate to this day. Again, we see the child of immeasurable wealth temporarily fallen into poverty. Only through bitter struggles did Xuefeng have such a sweet awakening. The conversation continued . . .

> *Xuefeng said, "Later on, I asked Deshan, 'Can a student understand the ancient teachings?' He struck me and said, 'What did you say?' At that moment it was like the bottom falling out of a bucket of water."*
>
> *Yantou said, "Haven't you heard it said that 'what comes in through the front gate isn't the family jewels?'"*

And so, for a third time, Xuefeng expresses his understanding by overlooking what's right in front of him and reaching back to another time and place. This person, this great bodhisattva, needs help. He recounts that when Deshan struck him, "it was like the bottom falling out of a bucket of water." One, two, three strikes, he's out. For Yantou, that was more than enough such missed opportunities.

> *Xuefeng said, "Then, in the future, what should I do?"*
>
> *Yantou said, "In the future, if you want to expound a great teaching, then it must flow forth from your own breast. In the future, your teaching and mine will cover heaven and earth."*
>
> *When Xuefeng heard this, he experienced unsurpassed awakening. He then bowed and said, "Elder Brother,[15] at last today on Tortoise Mountain, I've attained the Path!"*

So now we see that for a person to be just a person is precisely to experience unsurpassed, authentic awakening. With Yantou's fierce encouragement, Xuefeng was finally able to give up searching outside, and he realized the stage of person. Finally, he gave up trying to bring the family jewels in through the front gate. He just let awakening flow forth from his breast and cover heaven and earth. From that time on, he was available to all sentient beings. It may seem unusual that it is Xuefeng's dharma brother Yantou who brings his practice to maturity although all those previous masters were not able to do so. I am deeply touched by Yantou's loving-kindness and great compassion as it is expressed in this story.

Our true nature is always present and supporting us. This is not only true for monks and nuns on pilgrimage but also for laypeople living their daily life. Whether monastic or lay, we can be mindful that the profound knowledge of our original nature is our constant companion. Xuefeng scolded Yantou for sleeping all day. Xuefeng didn't understand that whether we are standing, sitting, walking, or lying down and sleeping, our true nature is never separate from us. Xuefeng never cheated himself by being lazy; he cheated himself by diligently looking someplace else for himself. Xuefeng was afraid of cheating or deceiving himself. But, in fact, he had been doing just that for a long time. While he faithfully followed what he believed to be the path of true knowledge by seeking it somewhere else, he simultaneously walked away from it and cheated himself of it. How sad. No wonder he felt anxious. We, too, will be anxious if we seek outside.

Xuefeng was a person on the path of profound knowledge. He was richly endowed with enthusiasm for great awakening.

Only someone who was so rich could fall into such deep poverty. After many years of arduous effort, he was finally able to allow himself to be an ordinary person, without seeking anything. He realized that an ordinary person is neither conjoined with nor separate from great awakening. Thus, he realized his original nature.

Xuefeng and Yantou's stories show us that the work of making a Zen master is actualized by thoroughly *not* being a Zen master. Xuefeng was really good at seeking outside himself and not being a Zen master. Thus, he gave us one of the great moments of Zen history. The ramifications of this gift are forever fresh and still to be enjoyed. Do you see the jewels hidden in this story of their relationship? Do you see the jewels hidden within your own heart?

13

Bursting Out of the Clear Sky

WE HAVE EXPLORED THE BODHISATTVA PATH within the framework of a parable along with many old and new stories. At the end of the parable, when the poor son heard his father's words and realized his inheritance and received something he had never had before, he was filled with joy. He thought, "Without any intention or effort on my part, these treasures have now come to me of themselves." However, the parable doesn't tell us how the son lived after joyfully receiving his inheritance. But now we will contemplate how the life of the bodhisattva vow flows forth from and goes beyond this deep and vast inheritance.

The following stories illustrate some possibilities in the intimate succession of awakening in which our family business is inherited, transcended, and transmitted to the next generation. To fully protect, nourish, and maintain a living tradition, it is also necessary to lovingly allow it to change so that it may adapt and flourish under ever-changing circumstances. These changes flow forth best from our devotion and commitment to the traditional bodhisattva vows and from our openness to questioning and being questioned.

In the Zen tradition, one of the ways students and teachers work together to protect and maintain the lineage is by conducting ceremonies for their ancestors. Performing these rituals is also a way that we create opportunities to contemplate and question the teachings.

The following two stories celebrate and transmit Yunyan's teaching and probe its depths. The students in both stories show us the possibility of respectfully disagreeing with our teacher. In the first story a student even questions whether Yunyan understood his own teaching.

> *Once during a memorial ceremony, Dongshan was making offerings to a portrait of Yunyan when a monk asked, "Yunyan said, 'Just this person,' did he not?"*
>
> *Dongshan said, "Yes."*
>
> *The monk asked, "What was his meaning?"*
>
> *Dongshan said, "Back then I almost misunderstood my teacher's meaning."*
>
> *The monk said, "I'd like to know if Yunyan really knew this or not."*
>
> *Dongshan said, "If he didn't know, how could he speak in this manner? And if he did know, why was he willing to speak this way?"*[1]

As far as I know, the teaching of "just this person" that Yunyan entrusted to Dongshan is unprecedented. It is a great innovation in the history of the buddha way. Now we have a monk questioning whether Dongshan's teacher, Yunyan, understood his own teaching! Dongshan says, "If he didn't know, how could he speak in this manner? And if he did know, why was he willing to speak this way?" How could these unprecedented words come out of the mouth of someone who didn't understand? People can say a lot of things that they don't understand, but the proposal here is that the first person to say it is someone who understands.

On the other hand, if one understands this teaching, why would it be necessary or helpful to say it? Yunyan compassionately stated this profound truth for Dongshan and us because we need to hear it to understand it. Day after day we go together with Yunyan and Dongshan deeper into the mystery.

During another memorial ceremony that Dongshan was conducting for Yunyan, a monk asked, "What teaching did you receive when you were at Yunyan's place?"

The master said, "Although I was there, I didn't receive any teaching."

"Since you didn't actually receive any teaching, why are you conducting this memorial?" asked the monk.

"Why should I turn my back on him?" said the master.

"If you began by meeting Nanquan, why do you now conduct a memorial for Yunyan?" asked the monk.

"It's not my former master's virtue or buddhadharma that I esteem, only that he did not make exhaustive explanations for me," replied the master.

"Since you are conducting this memorial for the former master, do you agree with him or not?" asked the monk.

The master said, "I agree with half and don't agree with half."

"Why don't you agree with him completely?" asked the monk.

The master said, "If I agreed completely, then I would be ungrateful to my former master."[2]

We may wish to completely agree with our teacher, but Dongshan suggests that having no possibility of disagreement might not be true intimacy. Complete agreement might miss some of the irony of Yunyan's teaching. This could be why Yunyan did not give Dongshan exhaustive explanations. We might think that coming into accord with our teachers leaves no room for disagreement but, ironically, true intimacy may require some disagreement with our teacher. Dongshan and his successors for more than a thousand years have continued to take care of the irony of this intimacy. And isn't it ironic that one might wholeheartedly wish to realize "just this person" even though one doesn't know for sure who or what this person is?

In my case, although I wanted to study and learn from Suzuki Roshi, I was not interested in completely agreeing with him. However, I was concerned that I might be agreeing with him too much. After hearing and reading old Zen stories about student-teacher relationships that involved considerable difficulty and disagreement, I wondered if I was missing something with Suzuki Roshi because I felt so little difficulty or disagreement with him. So I brought this up with him. He said, "Later we will have difficulty." As it turned out, he died before we had any real difficulty with each other. Now, although I wouldn't say I disagree with him, as I study transcripts and recordings of his teachings, I sometimes wonder what he meant and really wish I could explore these questions with him.

One time it seemed like the whole sangha disagreed with Suzuki Roshi. During a sesshin in the last year of his life, the wake-up bell was rung an hour early. Hearing the bell, I got up, put on my robes and, as I stepped out of the door of my room, I saw Suzuki Roshi walk by on his way to the meditation hall. He went to the meditation hall and sat waiting for us to arrive. But we didn't come because the person who rang the wake-up bell noticed his mistake and went around the halls of the building telling us that the bell was rung early, and we could go back to bed. Most of us did, including me. After a while Suzuki Roshi realized we weren't coming, and he went back to his room. An hour later, the bell was rung again, and we all went to the meditation hall to sit.

After we were all seated in the meditation hall, Suzuki Roshi described what had happened: The bell was rung early, we got up, heard that it was early, and went back to bed. Then he shouted, "What do you think we are doing here!" He got up from his seat with his stick and hit each of us. Since I was sitting closest to him, he hit me first with all of his might. I could hear him grunt with effort. He then proceeded to hit every person sitting in the meditation hall. Toward the end, the hits were much softer. He completely exhausted himself in giving us this teaching. I don't remember now if I was crying at the end, but I was deeply moved by his kindness and love for us.

Although I didn't experience strong disagreement with Suzuki Roshi during his lifetime, almost twenty years after he died, while I was an abbot at Zen Center, in accordance with the circumstances of the times, I endeavored to transmit Suzuki Roshi's stick of compassion by discontinuing its use.

At Green Dragon Zen Temple where I have lived for about fifty years, we had a tearoom that eventually became a teahouse with a walled garden. Several decades ago, we had the good fortune to study a tea ceremony in that tearoom with a tea teacher named Nakamura Sensei.

The teaching of "just this person" was embodied in the way she taught. Once, when we were sitting in the tearoom, I saw a scroll of Chinese calligraphy that she had hung in the alcove. The calligraphy said in Japanese, *buji kore kinnin.* This may be literally translated as "having nothing is a noble person," which is another way of saying "just this person." This spirit is at the heart of Zen and the practice of tea.

Nakamura Sensei was very perceptive at noticing if people were bringing anything extra into the tearoom. Some of the tea students came to the practice having already learned various arts and physical skills, which they brought into the room. She encouraged us to give up our previously acquired skills inside the tearoom and, as much as possible, to check our skills at the door. For example, some who came were well-trained pianists or ballet dancers. When the pianists went to pick up a tea implement to prepare tea, they had a dramatic way of touching the implement as though they were touching the keys of a piano. They brought a piano player's way into the tea ceremony. The ballet dancers had a graceful, studied way of moving, which they carried into the room. It was lovely to behold. But the tea teacher said it was not the way of tea. They were bringing a style they possessed into the room. Now, in the tearoom, they were asked to give up the beauty of their style of piano playing and ballet dancing. As part of the ceremony, we learn new formal ways of walking, standing, kneeling, and sitting in the tearoom. When one learns to sit in the tearoom, it is not that there is sitting plus the person doing the sitting. There is just sitting.

This is hard for us to learn. Everyone has to give up something to become a true person who is not possessive of anything. Whatever it is, after we give it up, we enter the way of Zen, the way of tea. The spirit of Zen and the spirit of tea is to not bring anything into the room.

In the spirit of the bodhisattva precept of not being possessive of anything, we study tea and we study Zen. We give up doing things in our habitual ways and learn the way of tea. After learning one of the formal ways of making tea, we are encouraged to let that go too. After thoroughly training in this way, we realize the person who has nothing. Even so, we continue to practice tea ceremony, and we don't even possess a teacher or a student. There is just the tea ceremony. Here, in the radical simplicity of Nakamura Sensei's teaching, the noble person who is not possessive of anything, is present. Her way of teaching reminds me of Yangshan's teaching of the three mysteries.

Suzuki Roshi gave us the dharma, the practice of just sitting, and the bodhisattva precepts. In the ceremony of giving and receiving the bodhisattva precepts, he also gave us a document titled "Serene Name" in which our dharma names were written. In these names he embedded the teaching of "just this person." In homage to him, his successors in this lineage continue the practice of transmitting the bodhisattva precepts and giving dharma names that embody teachings. These names, like all phenomena, are not fixed or static things. They are constantly evolving, and they contain boundless universes. As we live and practice with our dharma names, we will discover this.

Since receiving a dharma name, my understanding of it has been continuously evolving. I have been practicing with the teachings embedded in this name, awakening to their import, and transmitting them. Over the years, I have discovered that this gift is endlessly deep and wide. The teachings contained within this name continue to unfold and surprise me. They yield fresh revelations, and I don't know if I will ever come to the end of them.

As I said before, the name Suzuki Roshi gave me is Tenshin Zenki. Although he gave this name to me, it's not just for me. It is for everyone. Therefore, I am sharing this gift with you.

When he gave me that name, Suzuki Roshi also said, "*Tenshin* means 'Reb is Reb.'" Then he added, "People may have some problem with that, but it can't be helped." He said that our practice is to be completely ourselves in each moment without expecting anything. This teaching of tenshin, "you are you," cannot be avoided, no matter how hard we try. And people may have some problems with us as we struggle to practice this.

Shortly after receiving this name, I showed it to a Japanese person who was teaching me how to write Chinese characters. When he saw the characters for my name, he said, "Oh, your name means 'just sitting' (*shikantaza*); your name is zazen." At that time, I was surprised to hear that interpretation, which I had not seen or heard before. It was like the story in the *Lotus Sutra* where a rich person sewed a precious jewel into the robes of a poor friend who was drunk and asleep.

Now I was beginning to get a glimmer of the jewels sewn into the name that had been given to me when I was drunk with delusion. I needed help to fully appreciate what was transmitted to me. I knew that I had been given something precious in the form of this dharma name, but I did not realize the full extent of its worth.

At the time he gave me the name, I don't remember Suzuki Roshi saying anything directly about the second part of the name, Zenki. At that time, I didn't know what *zenki* meant. Later, I learned that *zenki* can be translated into English as "total dynamic working" or "the whole works." I like the translation "the whole works" because it has both a colloquial and a standard meaning that pivot on each other. Colloquially, "the whole works" is a statement meaning everything or the whole universe. In standard English, it is a complete sentence. The whole works. How does it work? The whole universe works through each thing being completely itself, and each thing being completely itself is the working of the whole universe. Now I see that Suzuki Roshi lived each moment of his life as the whole works and showed us how to live that way.

In his essay "The Whole Works" ("Zenki"), Dogen says, "[It's] like riding in a boat. You raise the sails and you row the boat. Although you do the rowing, the boat gives you a ride. And without the boat, no one can ride. You ride in the boat and your riding makes the boat a boat. You should meditate on this precise point."[3] In truth, we are the whole works.

Learning about the teachings embedded in this name is an ongoing process of amazement and discovery. As I have grown older and sobered up from my youthful ignorance,

I have realized more of its boundless virtue, and I vow to remember, contemplate, and share it.

Now I see the thread of this teaching—*tenshin zenki*—running through almost all the stories that we have considered so far.

As we saw in the previous chapter, the dynamic and intimate relationship of Yantou and Xuefeng reveals the inner workings of the teaching of tenshin zenki. Within the wondrous workings of their friendship, a central teaching of the *Lotus Sutra* also shines forth. This is the teaching that only buddha together with buddha can exhaustively investigate the reality of all things. This teaching embraces both "only buddha" (tenshin) and "together with buddha" (zenki).

"Only buddha" is our wholehearted practice of just sitting. It is each of us being "just this person." It is the difficult work of settling completely into who we are in each moment and fully accepting responsibility for that. Buddhas demonstrate settling completely in each moment. This is being completely a fool when we are a fool. Xuefeng was really good at "Xuefeng is Xuefeng." He was really tenshin.

Then the *Lotus Sutra* adds "together with buddha." This is the social practice of all solitary buddhas. Buddha's solitary practice and social practice are in perfect harmony. The intimate relationship of Xuefeng and Yantou wonderfully demonstrates this. They needed each other to realize the reality of all phenomena.

Not only is the teaching of tenshin zenki running through all the stories we have considered, but it is also present in the *Lotus Sutra*. "Only buddha together with buddha" runs through the words *tenshin* and *zenki* and vice versa. This name is one of Suzuki Roshi's innovative, and perhaps unprecedented, ways of expressing the teaching that only buddha together with buddha can thoroughly comprehend the reality of all things.

The discovery that this essential teaching of the *Lotus Sutra* is hidden in this name—Tenshin Zenki—is another unfoldment of the teaching of all buddhas. The solitary practice of "only buddha" is the practice of "Reb is Reb" and "you are you." This is being a solitary buddha. This is tenshin.

Then the *Lotus Sutra* says, "together with buddha." This is the social practice of all solitary buddhas. Herein we are practicing together and being included in each other. In this way we unconditionally support others and are supported by them. When we fully accept and allow this mutual inclusion, we are realizing buddhas' work. *Zenki* is "*together* with buddha" and buddha together with us. It is the intimate relationship of each solitary buddha with every other solitary buddha. It is you being you *together* with me being me. When the *Lotus Sutra* says "only buddha together with buddha," it is saying that when we are fully responsible for being "just this person," we realize that we are already intimately engaged with the whole universe. This is our inconceivable, imperceptible, original nature and our true home. This is the whole works, zenki.

During a sesshin in the spring of Suzuki Roshi's last year with us, he told a story about an esteemed teacher named Oka Sotan Roshi who was the teacher for a whole generation of Zen teachers. Once when I was talking to Suzuki Roshi in the courtyard of Zen Center, he told me the names of the many teachers who were students of Oka Sotan. While he was telling me this, I made a chart of all these names. I wrote them down in some blank pages at the back of a Buddhist Sanskrit-English dictionary I happened to have with me. I still have that dictionary. Among Oka Sotan's students were Suzuki Roshi's root teacher Gyokujun So-on, his biological father Butsumon Sogaku, his second teacher Kishizawa Ian, Sawaki Kodo, Hashimoto Eko, and many others, along with their students. So, Oka Sotan was the teacher of a whole generation of teachers. Suzuki Roshi said that most of his understanding of the bodhisattva precepts comes from Oka Sotan. Oka Sotan taught us how the bodhisattva precepts, like our dharma names, are not what we think they are. They contain and emit the boundless light of buddha's wisdom. Here's the story Suzuki Roshi told:

> *When Oka Sotan was a child living in a monastery, he was sent to the store to buy some tofu for dinner. On the way to the store, he stopped to gaze at one of those colorful woodblock prints that were used in those days to advertise Kabuki theater and circuses. He lost track of time and, when he heard the bell for the evening service that precedes dinner, he realized he would be late and ran quickly to the store.*
>
> *He said to the storekeeper, "Give it to me!"*
>
> *The man said, "What?"*
>
> *Little Sotan said, "The tofu!"*
>
> *The man gave him the tofu, and he ran back toward the monastery. But before he got there, he noticed that he had forgotten his hat.*

So, he turned about and ran back to the store and said to the man, "Give it to me!"

The man said, "What?"

He said, "My hat!"

The man said, "It's on your head," and Sotan ran back to the monastery.[4]

I can imagine myself doing something like this too. This is the ordinary, childlike activity of our lives, and it is also a manifestation of ultimate reality. This story is another jewel Suzuki Roshi sewed into our robes not only because it is a story about an influential Zen master, but also because it's a story about a foolish boy.

After he told this story, Suzuki Roshi said, "He was a very good boy." I was surprised by that and wondered what he meant by saying it. I could see that Sotan was a rather foolish, naughty boy, but I didn't see how he was good. Perhaps Suzuki Roshi saw that this boy was also a future buddha. Now I see that not only did this boy grow up to be a big Zen buddha; he was already a little Zen buddha. Do you see the buddha in the boy? Now we can see that he was both an unaffected child and a manifestation of ultimate reality. He was really tenshin.

In these stories we have told, we see how all our buddha ancestors continued to work with and transmit the teachings that they received and inherited from their teachers. These stories are gifts of the simple and profound teaching of intimacy. The never-ending work of receiving and transmitting the teaching of our original nature is our family business.

Although they preceded him, all the teachers we have spoken of awoke to Suzuki Roshi's teaching of tenshin zenki before he gave it to me. He intended this teaching for all of us—past, present, and future. We always have tenshin zenki within us, that is to say that no matter what we are experiencing, we always have the zazen of "just sitting" within us. This is our original nature. The ancestors serve as midwives in the delivery of this original nature. Suzuki Roshi and all our buddha ancestors planted this in all the teachings that they gave us. He, together with all his friends and teachers, shows us that this teaching is always with us. Just like our great ancestors, all people, including you and me, carry on this teaching in every moment of our lives. I wonder what further revelations are present in this teaching.

Celebrating the teaching of the ocean of all-knowing wisdom, its inheritance, and going beyond it, the Old Buddha Hongzhi said:

> *Bursting out of the clear sky, the garuda takes wing on the wind;*
> *Treading over the blue sea, thunder follows the roaming dragon.*[5]

Bodhisattvas have nothing to attain and everything to realize. They *are* great realization, and because the realization is great, it leaps beyond itself and leaves no trace. And this no trace goes on endlessly.

EPILOGUE

On the journey of discovering our original nature,
The Lotus Sutra *comes forth to embrace and sustain us.*
The parable of the destitute child illuminates our path
of return and realization,
Giving myriad job assignments to heiresses and heirs
of the true dharma.
"Only buddha together with buddha" is the heart
and soul of the sutra.
It is our family inheritance.
This sutra embraces and runs through all sutras.
It is a womb of bodhisattva practice.
Our compassionate ancestors' midwife our practice
from its boundless womb.

Our family business is born of these teachings
And goes far beyond them.
The myriad practice lineages flowing from the Lotus Sutra
Are like boundless waterfalls.
Old Guishan and Yangshan show us how to probe
and test our dung

For the immutable knowledge of all buddhas.
Yangshan offers face-to-face teaching
of mind and environment
To express the sweet dew of "only buddha together
with buddha."
Yunyan transmits this with Dongshan
In the fresh flower of "just this person."
In the night, Shiji visits Juzhi and plants a question.
Tianlong raises one finger and brings the question to fruition.
Daowu uses receiving and drinking tea to teach
Longtan the essential pivot of mind.
Longtan shows Deshan the light in the dark of the night.
Light flows from Deshan to bloom in the hearts
of Xuefeng and Yantou.
Their light now covers the whole earth.

Suzuki Roshi sews jewels into the fabric of our life.
He entrusts them to us to care for and share for
the welfare of the world,
For the mountains, the rivers, the grasses, and trees,
And for all living beings.

NOTES

INTRODUCTION: THE PARABLE OF THE DESTITUTE CHILD

1. The central text of the Huayen school of East Asian Buddhism, which had a profound and pervasive influence on the development of the Zen school.
2. Author's version of a parable in chapter 4 of the *Lotus Sutra*. The title of this chapter may be translated as "Faith and Understanding."
3. Eihei Dogen, 1200–1253 C.E.
4. From "Genjo Koan," San Francisco Zen Center liturgy, https://www.sfzc.org/files/daily_sutras_Genjo_Koan.

CHAPTER 1. THE BLOOMING OF THE *LOTUS SUTRA* IN ZEN TRAINING

1. Referring to a line from "Song of the Jewel Mirror Samadhi."
2. Mazu Daoyi (Japanese: *Baso Doitsu*), 709–788 C.E.
3. Author's version of a story about Mazu in Andrew Ferguson's *Zen's Chinese Heritage* (Wisdom Publications, 2011).

CHAPTER 2. THE PATH OF BUDDHA

1. Tiantong Hongzhi Zhengjue (Japanese: *Tendai Wanshi Shogaku*), 1091–1153 C.E.
2. See also Reb Anderson, *Entering the Mind of Buddha* (Shambhala Publications, 2019), 48, for another way to look at this story related to the paramita of ethics and buddha-nature precepts.

3. Dongshan Liangjie (Japanese: *Tozan Ryokai*), 807–869 C.E., is the founder of the Caedong school of Buddhism in China that became the Soto Zen lineage in Japan. *Liangje* means "good servant."
4. Thomas Cleary, trans., "Case 56," in *Book of Serenity: One Hundred Zen Dialogues* (Shambhala Publications, 1998), 237.
5. Zhaozhou Congshen (Japanese: *Joshu Jushin*), 778–897 C.E.
6. Author's version of Case 18 in the *Book of Serenity*.

CHAPTER 3. WANDERING AWAY

1. Eijun Linda Ruth Cutts, "Senjo and Her Soul Are Separated," in *The Hidden Lamp*, ed. Florence Caplow and Susan Moon (Wisdom Publications, 2013), 157.
2. Cutts, "Senjo and Her Soul Are Separated," 158.
3. Hakuin Ekaku, 1686–1769 C.E.
4. Paul Reps and Nyogen Senzaki, comp., *Zen Flesh, Zen Bones: A Collection of Zen and Pre-Zen Writings* (Tuttle Publishing, 1973), 22.
5. One of the three practices centers of the San Francisco Zen Center.
6. *Life* magazine, 1954, issue date unknown. It was a photograph of the noted Zen Buddhist scholar and philosopher Hisamatsu Shinichi, whose deep philosophical thought was embodied in his posture.

CHAPTER 4. DIVING DEEPLY INTO TRAINING

1. San Francisco Zen Center was founded by Shunryu Suzuki Roshi and includes three practice centers in California: City Center in San Francisco, Tassajara Zen Mountain Monastery in the Ventana Wilderness, and Green Gulch Zen Farm near Muir Beach.
2. This is one of the author's renditions of the bodhisattva precepts. For further discussion of the bodhisattva precepts in Zen training, see Reb Anderson, *Being Upright: Zen Meditation and the Bodhisattva Precepts* (Shambhala Publications, 2001).
3. Yunyan Tansheng (Japanese: *Ungan Donjo*), 780–841 C.E. Dongshan was his most important dharma heir.
4. William F. Powell, trans., *The Record of Tung-shan* (University of Hawai'i

Press, 1986), 26. The character used by Dongshan in this verse is the same as the character used for *dung* in the *Lotus Sutra*.

5. Author's version of a story told in a chapter about Liangshan in Zen Master Keizan's *Transmission of the Light* ("Denkoroku").
6. For further discussion of the practice of mindfulness, posture, breathing, and the pitfalls of attempting to control ourselves during the practice of concentration, see Reb Anderson, *Entering the Mind of Buddha: Zen and the Six Heroic Practices of Bodhisattvas* (Shambhala Publications, 2019), 87–88.

CHAPTER 5. UNFOLDING THE GIFT OF THE ROBE

1. Sokoji is a temple that was established to serve the Japanese American community in San Francisco. Suzuki Roshi came to the United States in 1959 to serve as a priest there.
2. *Okusan* (Japanese) is a respectful way to refer to someone's wife. *Oka* refers to the heart or the interior of the house.
3. T. S. Eliot, "The Dry Salvages," in *Four Quartets*, part 2 (Harcourt, 1943), 19.
4. Yuanwu Keqin (Japanese: *Engo Kokugon*), 1063–1135 C.E., was the commentator of the *Blue Cliff Record*. After studying with various teachers, he became the dharma heir to Wuzu Fayan of the Linji school.
5. The Chinese characters literally mean "red heart," but here they are understood to mean "upright" or "genuine" heart.
6. Author's version of Dogen's essay "Body-Mind Study of the Way" (Japanese: "Shinjingakudo"), in *Treasury of the True Dharma Eye* (Japanese: "Shobogenzo").
7. William R. Lafleur, trans., *Mirror for the Moon: A Collection of Poems by Saigyo* (New Directions Publications, 1977), 16.

CHAPTER 6. ENTERING THE HOUSE

1. "Guidelines for Studying the Way" (Japanese: "Gakudo Yojinshu"), in *Moon in a Dewdrop: Writings of Zen Master Dogen*, ed. and trans. Kazuaki Tanahashi (North Point Press, 1995), 43.

2. Nargajuna, approximately 150–250 C.E. Words cannot reach the vastness and depth of this teacher's wisdom and compassion.
3. Dajian Huineng (Japanese: *Daikan Eno*), 638–713 C.E., is called the Sixth Ancestor of Zen. He is a seminal figure for many lineages of Zen in China. According to tradition, he was an uneducated layperson who suddenly attained awakening upon hearing the chanting of the *Diamond Sutra* while walking around in a marketplace. Later he went to visit the Fifth Ancestor, Daman Hongren (Japanese: *Dajian Gunin*), 601–674 C.E., and became his successor.
4. Author's version of Dogen's essay "Dharma Flower Turns Dharma Flower" (Japanese: "Hokke Ten Hokke") in *Treasury of the True Dharma Eye* (Japanese: "Shobogenzo").

CHAPTER 7. COMPASSIONATELY STUDYING KARMIC CONSCIOUSNESS

1. From "Song of the Jewel Mirror Samadhi," San Francisco Zen Center liturgy, www.sfzc.org/files/daily_sutras_Song_of_the_Jewel_Mirror_Samadhi.
2. Guishan Lingyu (Japanese: *Isan Reiyu*), 771–853 C.E., and Yangshan Huiji (Japanese: *Kyozan Ejaku*), 807–883 C.E.
3. The word *monk* as used in this story and elsewhere throughout this manuscript should be understood as referring to both female and male monastics.
4. Thomas Cleary, trans., "Case 37," in *Book of Serenity: One Hundred Zen Dialogues* (Shambhala Publications, 1998), 163.
5. Author's version of Case 37 in the *Book of Serenity.*
6. Miaoxin (Japanese: *Myoshin*), 840–895 C.E., was a successor in the tradition of Guishan and Yangshan.
7. Kazuaki Tanahashi, ed., "Receiving the Marrow by Bowing," in *The Treasury of the True Dharma Eye: Zen Master Dogen's Shobogenzo*, vol. 1 (Shambhala Publications, 2010), 76.

CHAPTER 8. EXPLORING MIND AND ENVIRONMENT

1. Thomas Cleary, trans., "Case 32," in *Book of Serenity: One Hundred Zen Dialogues* (Shambhala Publications, 1998), 140.
2. In French, the word for ocean (*mer*) is contained in the word for mother (*mère*). Similarly, the Chinese character for *ocean* also contains the Chinese character for *mother*.

CHAPTER 9. THE PIVOTAL ACTIVITY OF ALL BUDDHAS

1. The Saha world refers to the world of suffering. The Sanskrit word *Saha* may be translated as "patience" or "endurance."
2. Author's version of a story in Case 32 in the *Book of Serenity*.
3. From "Fukanzazengi of Ehei Dogen," San Francisco Zen Center liturgy, www.sfzc.org/files/daily_sutras_Fukanzazengi.
4. Yaoshan Weiyan (Japanese: *Yakusen Igen*), 745–825 C.E.
5. Author's version of a poem in Dogen's essay "The Acupuncture Needle of Zazen" (Japanese: "Zazenshin"), in *Treasury of the True Dharma Eye* (Japanese: "Shobogenzo").
6. Author' version, "Acupuncture Needle."
7. Bodhidharma is a name often used to refer to the founder of the Chan, or Zen, tradition, who is often said to have transmitted Buddhist teachings from India to China. Who or what this founder actually is remains a great mystery.
8. Author's version of a story about Huike in chapter 30 of Zen Master Keizan's *Transmission of the Light* (Japanese: "Denkoroku").
9. From "Fukanzazengi of Eihei Dogen," San Francisco Zen Center liturgy, www.sfzc.org/files/daily_sutras_Fukanzazengi.

CHAPTER 10. THE STAGE OF FAITH

1. Shohaku Okumura, trans., "Wondrous Mind of Nirvana," in *Zen of Four Seasons: Dogen Zenji's Waka*, published by the Dogen Institute, www.dogeninstitute.wordpress.com/2015/01/02/zen-of-four-seasons-d.

CHAPTER 11. THE THREE MYSTERIES

1. Author's translation with Kazuaki Tanahashi of a story told by Kishizawa Ian in *Busso shoden shokawa* (Lectures on the Buddha ancestors correctly transmitted Zen precepts) vol. 2 (Soto School Headquarters, 1974), 7.
2. Tathagatha is one of the ten epithets of Buddha. It is often translated as "Thus Come One" or "Thus Gone One." It may be understood as one who has come from the realization of thusness or one who has gone to the realization of thusness.
3. The four-fold assembly refers to the four types of disciples: monks, nuns, laymen, and laywomen (Sanskrit: *bhiksus, bhiksunis, upasakas,* and *upasikas*).
4. Gene Reeves, trans., "Teachers of the Dharma," chapter 10 in *The Lotus Sutra: A Contemporary Translation of a Buddhist Classic* (Wisdom Publications, 2008), 231.
5. From "Short Verses," San Francisco Zen Center liturgy, https://www.sfzc.org/files/daily_sutras_short_verses.
6. Tiantai Deshao (Japanese: *Tendai Tokusho*). 891–972 C.E.
7. Thomas Cleary, trans., "Case 32," in *Book of Serenity: One Hundred Zen Dialogues* (Shambhala Publications, 1998), 144.

CHAPTER 12. REALIZING THE STAGE OF PERSON

1. Author's translation from "The Record of Dongshan" (Japanese: "Dongshanlu").
2. William Powell, trans., *Record of Tung-Shan* (University of Hawai'i Press, 1986), 27–28.
3. Jinhua Juzhi (Japanese: *Gutei*), ninth century. *Juzhi* is a transliteration of the Sanskrit word *koti*, which means "ten million." Ten Million was a nickname given to him by his dharma friends because he recited a Buddhist dharani called "Seventy Million Buddha Mothers." It was an incantation to great awakening. Perhaps he recited it millions of times.
4. Author's version of Case 84 in the *Book of Serenity*.

5. Author's version of Case 84.
6. Longtan Chongxin (Japanese: *Ryotan Sushin*); ninth century, exact dates uncertain.
7. Tianhuang Daowu (Japanese: *Tenno Dogo*), 748–807 C.E.
8. Andrew Ferguson, *Zen's Chinese Heritage: The Masters and Their Teachings* (Wisdom Publications, 2011), 170–71.
9. Deshan Xuanjian (Japanese: *Tokusan Senken*), 782–865 C.E.
10. Ferguson, *Zen's Chinese Heritage*, 216.
11. Author's version continuing the story quoted above.
12. Xuefeng Yicun (Japanese: *Seppo Gison*), 822–908 C.E., and Yantou Quanhuo (Japanese: *Ganto Zenkatsu*), 828–887 C.E., were dharma siblings who studied with Deshan. The lineage of Xuefeng extends from Daowu to Longtan to Deshan to Yantou and Xuefeng. Daowu helped Longtan discover the family jewels hidden in daily life, which is "just this person." Longtan helped Deshan discover the light of dharma in the midst of darkness.
13. This series of stories about the adventures of Xuefeng and Yantou are from Ferguson, *Zen's Chinese Heritage*, 262–63.
14. Yanguan Qian (Japanese: *Engan Saian*), 750–842 C.E.
15. Although Xuefeng was actually six years older than Yantou, Yantou is considered the "elder brother," probably because Yantou was ordained as a monk before Xuefeng. In Buddhist tradition, the one who enters the monastery or is fully ordained first is the senior. This is true even if the junior monk or priest is much older than the senior one.

CHAPTER 13. BURSTING OUT OF THE CLEAR SKY

1. Author's translation from the "Record of Dongshan" (Japanese: "Dongshanlu").
2. Author's translation from the "Record of Dongshan" (Japanese: "Dongshanlu").
3. Author's version from Dogen's essay "The Whole Works" (Japanese: *Zenki*), in *Treasury of the True Dharma Eye* (Japanese: "Shobogenzo").

4. Reb Anderson, *Warm Smiles from Cold Mountains: Dharma Talks on Zen Meditation* (Rodmell Press, 1999), 26–27.
5. This is two lines of Hongzi's poem commenting on Yangshan's "Mind and Environment" (Case 32 in the *Book of Serenity*).

ABOUT THE AUTHOR

TENSHIN REB ANDERSON is a lineage-holder in the Soto Zen tradition. He began training with Shunryu Suzuki Roshi at the San Francisco Zen Center in 1967; he was ordained by him as a priest in 1970 and given the name *Tenshin Zenki* ("Naturally Real," "The Whole Works"). He received dharma transmission in 1983 and served as abbot of the Zen Center's three training centers (City Center, Green Gulch Farm, and Tassajara Zen Mountain Center) from 1986 to 1995. He is particularly interested in Buddhist yoga, philosophy, psychology, and the relationship of wisdom and compassion to the social and ecological crises of our times. Together with his friends, he founded No Abode Hermitage in Mill Valley, California, in 2002. Tenshin Roshi has retired to No Abode where he continues to offer teachings and practice opportunities. He leads meditation retreats and classes nationally and internationally. Other information, including his teaching schedule and video and audio recordings of many of his dharma talks, are available at www.rebanderson.org.

BOOKS BY REB ANDERSON

Warm Smiles from Cold Mountains:
Dharma Talks on Zen Meditation

Being Upright:
Zen Meditation and the Bodhisattva Precepts

The Third Turning of the Wheel:
Wisdom of the Samdhinirmochana Sutra

Entering the Mind of Buddha:
Zen and the Six Heroic Practices of Bodhisattvas